A BARTHOLOMEW MA

MORE WALKS
IN THE
PEAK DISTRICT

BY BRIAN SPENCER

British Library Cataloguing in Publication Data
Spencer, Brian *1931-*
    More walks in the Peak District.
    1. England. Peak District - Visitors' guides
    I. Title
    914.25'1104858
    ISBN 0-7028-0951-9

Published by Bartholomew, Duncan Street, Edinburgh EH9 1TA.
Printed by Bartholomew in Edinburgh, Scotland.

First edition 1990

Produced for Bartholomew
by Curtis Garratt Limited, The Old Vicarage,
Horton cum Studley, Oxford OX9 1BT

Typesetting and maps by Taurus Graphics

Layouts by Taurus Graphics

ISBN 0 7028 0951 9

CONTENTS

KEY MAP FOR THE WALKS

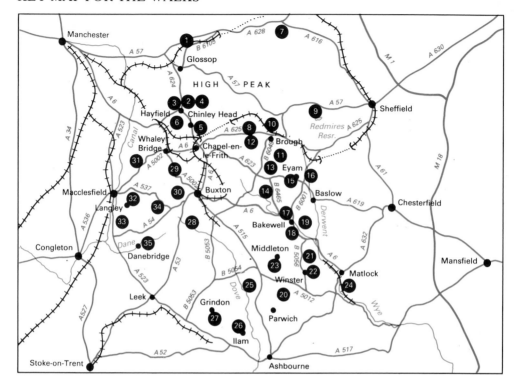

KEY TO SCALE AND MAP SYMBOLS

SCALE 1 : 63 360

SCALE 1 : 25 000

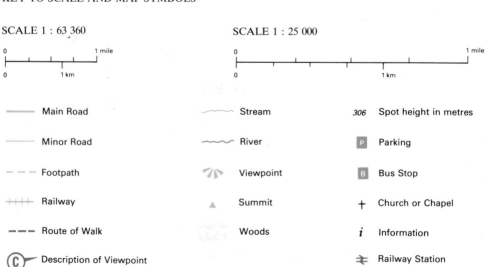

Main Road	Stream
Minor Road	River
Footpath	Viewpoint
Railway	Summit
Route of Walk	Woods
Description of Viewpoint	

306   Spot height in metres

P   Parking

B   Bus Stop

+   Church or Chapel

i   Information

⇌   Railway Station

1 WALKING IN THE PEAK DISTRICT

When walking in the Peak you can encounter four quite different types of terrain. Probably the easiest walking of all is on the limestone plateau where some stiles and green lanes indicate the way. In the dales, paths wander through shady woodland and follow bubbling trout rivers. In the north, the unpredictable weather makes navigation across the trackless moors quite difficult. Gritstone edges above the Derwent, or the lower heather moors, are more straightforward and the footpaths are easier to follow.

Walking is a sport which can fulfil the needs of everyone. You can adapt it to suit your own preferences and it is the healthiest of activities. Your inclination might be to walk two or three miles along a gentle track instead of one of the more arduous long-distance routes but, whatever the walk, it will always improve your general well-being. Walking should be anything from an individual pastime to a family stroll, or perhaps a group of friends enjoying the fresh air and open spaces of our countryside. There is no need for walking to be competitive and, to get the most from walking, it shouldn't be regarded simply as a means of covering a given distance in the shortest possible time.

As with all other outdoor activities, walking is safe provided a few simple common sense rules are followed.

(a) Make sure you are fit enough to complete the walk.

(b) Always try to let others know where you intend going.

(c) Be clothed adequately for the weather and always wear suitable footwear.

(d) Always allow plenty of time for the walk, especially if it is longer or harder than you have done before.

(e) Whatever the distance you plan to walk, always allow plenty of daylight hours unless you are absolutely certain of the route.

(f) If mist or bad weather come on unexpectedly, do not panic and try to remember the last certain feature which you have passed (road, farm, wood, etc). Then work out your route from that point on the map but be sure of your route before continuing.

(g) Do not dislodge stones on the high edges: there may be climbers or other walkers on the lower crags and slopes.

(h) Unfortunately, accidents can happen even on the easiest of walks. If this should be the case and you need the help of others, make sure that the injured person is safe in a place where no further injury is likely to occur. For example, the injured person should not be left on a steep hillside or in danger from falling rocks. If you cannot leave anyone with the injured person and, even if the person is conscious, try to leave a written note explaining the injuries and whatever you have done in the way of first-aid treatment. Make sure you know exactly where you left the person and then go to find assistance. If you meet a National Park Ranger, tell him or her what has happened. Otherwise, make your way to a telephone, dial 999, and ask for assistance. Unless the accident has happened within easy access of a road, then it is the responsibility of the Police to arrange evacuation. Always give accurate directions of how to find the casualty and, if possible, give an indication of the injuries involved.

(j) When walking in open country, learn to keep an eye on the immediate foreground while you admire the scenery or plan the route ahead. This may sound difficult, especially to a beginner but, once you can adapt to this method, your enjoyment will increase.

(k) It is best to walk at a steady pace, always on the flat of the feet because this is less tiring. Try not to walk directly up or downhill. A zig-zag route is a more comfortable way of negotiating a slope. Running directly downhill is a major cause of erosion on popular hillsides.

(l) When walking along a country road, walk on the right, facing the traffic. The exception to this rule is, when approaching a blind bend, the walker should cross over to the left and so have a clear view and also be seen in both directions.

(m) Finally, always park your car where it will not cause inconvenience to other road users or prevent a farmer from gaining access to his fields. Make sure that you lock your car and hide any valuables before leaving or, preferably, carry all valuables with you.

2 EQUIPMENT

Equipment, including clothing, footwear, and rucksacks, is essentially a personal thing and depends on several factors, such as the type of activity planned, the time of year, and weather likely to be encountered.

All too often, a novice walker will spend pounds on a fashionable jacket but will skimp when it comes to buying footwear or a comfortable rucksack. Blistered and tired feet quickly remove all enjoyment from even the most exciting walk and a poorly balanced rucksack will soon feel as though it is carrying half a hundreweight. Well-designed equipment is not only more comfortable but, being better made, it is longer lasting.

Clothing should be adequate for the day. In summer, remember to protect your head and neck, which are particularly vulnerable, in a strong sun. Wear light woollen socks, and lightweight boots or strong shoes will be adequate. A spare pullover and waterproofs carried in the rucksack should, however, always be there in case you need them.

Winter wear is a much more serious affair. Remember that, once the body starts to lose heat, it becomes much less efficient. Jeans are particularly unsuitable for winter wear and can sometimes even be downright dangerous.

It pays to buy the best waterproof clothing you can afford. Make sure that the jacket is loose-fitting, has a generous hood, and comes down at least to knee level. Waterproof overtrousers will not only offer complete protection in the rain but they are also windproof. Do not be misled by flimsy nylon 'showerproof' affairs. Remember, too, that garments made from rubberized or plastic material are heavy to carry and wear and they trap body condensation. Your rucksack should have wide, padded carrying straps for comfort.

It is important to wear boots that fit well or shoes with a good moulded sole – blisters can ruin any walk! Your clothes should be comfortable and not likely to catch on twigs and bushes. In winter, it is best to take two lightweight jumpers, one at least with a crew neck. You will find this better than wearing one jumper made of heavy material. Your jacket should have a hood and it should be windproof and loose enough for an extra layer of warmer clothing underneath. A woollen or thermofleece hat, which can be pulled well down, is essential in winter.

A piece of semi-rigid plastic foam carried in the rucksack makes a handy and yet almost weightless seat for open-air picnics.

An area map, as well as this guide, is useful for accurate navigation and it adds to the enjoyment of a walk. Finally, a small first-aid kit is an invaluable help in coping with cuts and other minor injuries.

3 PUBLIC RIGHTS OF WAY

Although most of the area covered by this guide comes within the authority of the Peak National Park, this does not mean that there is complete freedom of access to walk anywhere. Much of the land within the park is privately owned and what might appear to be an ideal spot for a picnic, or somewhere to exercise the dog, is often part of another person's livelihood.

In 1949, the National Parks and Access to the Countryside Act tidied up the law covering rights of way. Following public consultation, maps were drawn up by the Countryside Authorities of England and Wales to show all the rights of way.

Copies of these maps are available for public inspection and are invaluable when trying to resolve doubts over little-used footpaths. Once on the map, the right of way is irrefutable.

Right of way means that anyone may walk freely on a defined footpath or ride a horse or pedal cycle along a public bridleway. No-one may interfere with this right and the walker is within his or her rights to remove any obstruction along the route, provided that the walker has not set out purposely with the intention of removing that obstruction. All obstructions should be reported to the local Highways Authority.

Free access to footpaths and bridleways does mean that certain guidelines should be followed as courtesy to those who live and work in the area. For example, you should only sit down to picnic where it does not interfere with other walkers or the landowner. All gates must be closed to prevent stock from straying, and dogs must be kept under close control – usually this means that they should be kept on a leash. Motor vehicles must not be driven along a public footpath or bridleway without the landowner's consent.

A farmer can put a docile mature beef bull with a herd of cows or heifers in a field crossed by a public footpath. Beef bulls, such as Herefords, (usually brown/red colour) are unlikely to be upset by passers-by but dairy bulls, such as the black-and-white Friesian, can be dangerous by nature. It is, therefore, illegal for a farmer to let a dairy bull roam loose in a field open to public access.

Most public rights of way within the Peak National Park have been clearly defined and are marked as such on available maps. They are marked on the Ordnance Survey Landranger 1:50 000 maps as red dots for footpaths and red dashes for bridleways. The system is the same on the 1 inch (1:63 360) Tourist Map of the area which is still available. On the OS 1:25 000 scale, the dots and dashes are green. (Red dots and dashes on the 1:25 000 Outdoor Leisure Maps indicate permitted footpaths and bridleways respectively). All of the walks in this guide cover routes which follow public rights of way.

4 THE COUNTRY CODE

The Country Code has been designed not as a set of hard and fast rules – although they do have the backing of the law – but as a statement of common sense. The code is a gentle reminder of how to behave in the countryside. Walkers should walk with the intention of leaving the place exactly as it was before they arrived. There is an old saying that a good walker 'leaves only footprints and takes only photographs', which really sums up the code perfectly.

Never walk more than two abreast on a footpath as you will erode more ground and cause an unnatural widening of paths. Also try to avoid the spread of trodden ground around a boggy area. Mud can soon be cleaned from boots but plant life is slow to grow back once it has been worn away.

Have respect for everything in the countryside, be it those beautiful flowers found along the way or a farmer's gate which is difficult to close.

Stone walls were built at a time when labour costs were a fraction of those today, and the special skills required to build or repair them have almost disappeared. Never climb over or on to stone walls: always use stiles and gates.

Dogs which chase sheep can cause them to lose their lambs, and a farmer is within his rights if he shoots a dog which he believes is worrying his stock.

The moors and woodlands are often tinder dry in summer, so take care not to start a fire. A fire caused by something as simple as a discarded cigarette can burn for weeks, once it gets deep down into the underlying peat.

When walking across fields or enclosed land, make sure that you read the map carefully and avoid trespassing. As a rule, the line of a footpath or right of way, even when it is not clearly defined on the ground, can usually be followed by lining up stiles or gates.

5 MAP READING

Some people find map reading so easy that they can open a map and immediately relate it to the area of countryside in which they are standing. To others a map is as unintelligible as ancient Greek! A map is an accurate but flat picture of the three-dimensional features of the countryside. Features, such as roads, streams, woodlands, and buildings are relatively easy to identify, either from their shape or position.

Heights, on the other hand, can be difficult to interpret from the single dimension of a map. The 1:25 000 Pathfinder and 1:50 000 Landranger maps give the contours at 10-metre intervals. Summits and spot heights are also shown.

The best way to estimate the angle of a slope, as shown on any map, is to remember that, if the contour lines come close together, then the slope is steep – the closer the steeper.

Learn the symbols for features shown on the map and, when starting out on a walk, line up the map with one or more feature, recognizable both from the map and the ground. In this way the map will be correctly positioned relative to the terrain. It should only be necessary to look from the map towards the footpath or objective of your walk and then make for it! This process is also useful for determining your position at any time during the walk.

Let's take the skill of map reading one stage further: sometimes there are no easily recognizable features nearby: there may be the odd clump of trees and a building or two but none of them can be related exactly to the map. This is a frequent occurrence but there is a simple answer to the problem and this is where the use of a compass comes in. Simply place the map on the ground, or other flat surface, with the compass held gently above the map. Turn the map until the edge is parallel to the line of the compass needle, which should point to the top of the map. Lay the compass on the map and adjust the position of both, making sure that the compass needle still points to the top of the map and is parallel to the edge. By this method, the map is orientated in a north-south alignment. To find your position on the map, look out for prominent features and draw imaginary lines from them down on to the map. Your position is where these lines cross. This method of map reading takes a little practice before you can become proficient but it is worth the effort.

It is all too easy for members of a walking group to leave map reading to the skilled member or members of the party. No one is perfect and even the best map reader can make mistakes. Other members of the group should take the trouble to follow the route on the map, so that any errors are spotted before they cause problems.

Once you become proficient at map reading, you will learn to estimate the length of time required for a walk. Generally, you should estimate an extra five minutes for every 100 feet (30.5 m) you walk uphill.

6 THE PEAK DISTRICT NATIONAL PARK

In many other countries, National Parks are wilderness areas, where few people live unless they are connected with running the park. Countries such as the United States of America have even gone to the length of moving residents off land designated as a National Park. In England and Wales, National Parks are areas of outstanding beauty where people still live and work. One of the major functions of a National Park is to preserve the landscape and the livelihoods of the people living within its boundaries. This is achieved by careful planning control. The National Parks and Access to the Countryside Act of 1949 led to the formation of the nine National Parks in England and Wales. The Peak National Park was designated as such in 1951.

The word 'National' in the title sometimes leads to misunderstanding. National Parks are not 'nationalized' or in any way owned by the government. Most of the land within the park is privately owned by the people who live and work there – be they farmers, private landowners, or quarry owners. Certain areas of scenic beauty and ancient buildings around the Peak District are owned by The National Trust but these were left as gifts by far-sighted owners as a means of ensuring their preservation.

The Peak National Park extends over 542 square miles (1403 sq km). Divided into two uniquely different zones, with wild gritstone moors to the north and gentler limestone uplands and dales to the south, it is surrounded by millions of people living in the industrial areas of England. With the advent of motorways, the Peak is accessible to the bulk of the population in under two hours. The Peak District was the first National Park and is the most visited.

Administration of the park is controlled by a committee composed, on a proportional basis, of representatives of the surrounding County and Metropolitan Councils and two District Councils as well as members appointed by the Secretary of State for the Environment.

One of the statutory functions of a Park Authority is the appointment of full-time and voluntary Park Rangers. These are people with particular knowledge of some aspects of the local environment who are available to give help and advice to visitors. Other functions of the Ranger Service include giving assistance to local farmers in such matters as rebuilding damaged walls to prevent stock from straying and leading guided walks from Information Centres. Permanent Information Centres are based at Edale, Castleton, and Bakewell.

Probably the most important responsibility of the Peak National Park, from the point of view of the walker, is the negotiation of access agreements across open moorland. During the late 1920s and early 1930s, rambling grew in popularity as workers from the industrial towns looked for a means of escaping their crowded existence. The obvious place for this escape was to the high moors which were jealously guarded by their owners, who used them for grouse shooting. Pressures caused by the demand for easy and free access often led to conflicts of interest.

Several ramblers, mainly the alleged ring-leaders, were arrested and received sentences ranging from two to six months, but they had made their point. One of the first tasks the Peak National Park set itself after its formation in 1951 was to negotiate access agreements. These were not always straightforward but, by careful and diplomatic negotiation, agreements have been reached with farmers and landowners giving free access to most of the high moors of the Dark Peak. In all, a total of 76 square miles (197 sq km) of moorland, including Kinder Scout, are open to unrestricted walking and rock climbing apart from a few days in summer when sections of the moors are closed for grouse shooting. Notices are published locally showing the dates when the moors are closed and there are also signposts giving dates at access points to the moors.

Losehill Hall National Park Study Centre is a converted Victorian mansion which is set in spaciously wooded grounds to the south of Lose Hill. Residential and day courses are held on a wide variety of topics ranging from environmental studies, archaeology, and the National Park and the pressures it faces, to hill walking, cycling, caving, and more specialized subjects.

7 WHAT IS THE PEAK DISTRICT?

The title 'Peak District' is something of a misnomer. To begin with, there are only two or three hills in the district which can claim to represent the true conical shape of a peak. The name 'Peak', in fact, refers to a tribe who lived in the area in ancient times. In the year 924, a cleric writing about the hills and dales of what is now North Derbyshire, referred to the inhabitants as living in *Peaclond* and the name seems to have stuck. *Peac* comes from the Old English for knoll or hill: there is a hilly or mountainous meaning to the title, but certainly not 'peaks' in the strictest sense. Another Old English reference occurs in the use of 'low' which comes from *hlaw* meaning a mound or a hill. No wonder visitors are often confused – peaks where there are none and high points called lows!

There are really two Peak Districts – Dark and White. The two areas are so completely different that, when standing on the breezy limestone plateau of the White Peak, it is hard to imagine that the untamed wilderness of Bleaklow and Kinder Scout are not far away.

Broadly speaking, the Peak District can be subdivided into six distinct areas.
(a) The most northerly is the wildest, and covers the moors above Saddleworth and the Longdendale Valley with the huge spread of Bleaklow filling the space between Longdendale and the Snake Pass.
(b) Kinder Scout is a vast, boggy plateau bordered to its south by Edale and the graceful sweep of the Mam Tor/Rushup Edge Ridge.
(c) To the east, rising above the Derwent Valley, there is a long escarpment which is clearly defined by a series of gritstone edges backed by heather moorland.
(d) In the west, gritstone crags range from The Roaches above Leek to Windgather Rocks and Castle Naze on the northern limits. High open moors offer miles of lesser-known walking. Tranquil wooded valleys cutting the western moors are excellent places to walk on hot summer days.
(e) Limestone makes its most northerly appearance in dramatic cliffs and knolls above Castleton, a place of caves and ancient lead mines. South of Castleton are some of the highest villages in the White Peak. They can expect to be cut off by deep

snow for several days during most winters.

(f) The limestone plateau to the south-west of the A6 is incised by deep valleys and is judged by many to be the prettiest part of the Peak. It is certainly a zone of contrasts where the lush pastures of the rolling uplands have been grazed by cattle since time immemorial. Rivers run pure and clear, and they are full of lively trout.

People came early to the Peak. Settling first on the treeless limestone plateau, they left mysterious mounds and stone cirles. The circle at Arbor Low between Hartington and Youlgreave was probably the most important. Certainly its surrounding earthworks indicate its significance. Arbor Low is unique as the stones lie flat, unlike the more normal uprights associated with other circles. Early humans hunted in the Dark Peak, following the seasonal migrations of game across moorland then covered by scrubby birch and mountain ash. Oak trees filled most of the valleys and dales, and made them impregnable until later dwellers cut the trees for fuel and building material. During later and less settled eras, massive earthworks were constructed at different times on top of Mam Tor and at Carl Wark.

Lead brought the Romans into the Peak. The metal, which was mined long before their arrival, attracted them to the area and they established their main centre at *Lutadarum*. Lead ingots embossed with this name have been found, and an archaeological survey indicates that *Lutadarum* was probably near Wirksworth. Further north, a fort was built at *Navio* below the village of Hope, to control the hostile natives.

Following the Norman Conquest, the northern part of the Peak was designated a royal game forest or *frith* (hence Chapel-en-le-Frith).

William Peveril, illegitimate son of the Conquerer, had a castle built on an easily defendable crag above Castleton. The castle controlled the king's lead-mining interests as well as providing a base for hunting expeditions.

During the Middle Ages, most of the lands were owned by various monasteries. They continued to exploit the resources of lead which was then very much in demand both as a roofing material and for constructing pipes to supply water into a growing number of monastic establishments. The monks opened large tracts of arable grazing and produced wool to clothe an expanding population. Farms,

which today have the word Grange as part of their name, were owned by rich monasteries until the dissolution by Henry VIII.

Great houses have been built in the Peak. Some are well known, such as Chatsworth with its parkland which was landscaped by Capability Brown, or Haddon Hall – a uniquely preserved medieval country house. There are also many lesser-known stately homes throughout the district which are just as interesting. Most are in private hands; Tissington Hall has been owned by the same family for generations. Hartington Hall, a fine example of a Jacobean yeoman's house, is now a youth hostel as is Ilam Hall which is an early Victorian mansion preserved by the National Trust.

Customs and festivals abound in the Peak: a unique and charming custom is 'well dressing'. Pictures, usually of a biblical theme, are made from colourful petals, mosses, and twigs stuck on to wet clay. The origins of this delightful custom, which offers thanks for the plentiful supply of water on the dry limestone plateau, are lost in the mists of time. A dozen or so villages dress their wells each year, and details of the dates are included in the Peak Park's calendar of events. Local Shrovetide customs include the pancake race in Winster and a football match in Ashbourne where almost anything goes. A more tranquil custom is the Castleton Garland Procession. Although the procession is linked to ancient fertility rites, it always takes place on 29 May (Oak Apple Day) in commemoration of the restoration to the throne of Charles II. Also, the annual 'Love Feast' is held on the first Sunday in July in a barn in Alport Dale, high above Snake Road. This is a link with times when dissenting worshippers, who disagreed with the 'Act of Uniformity' tying them to the Church of England, had to find seclusion away from the attentions of the troops of the reinstated King Charles II. Forest Chapel, near Wildboarclough, has a rush-bearing ceremony on the Sunday nearest to 12 August each year.

Visitors to the Peak can buy jewellery made from Blue John, a semi-precious stone found only beneath Treak Cliff, near Castleton. Another Peak novelty is the Bakewell Pudding (never call it a tart!). This delicacy was first made accidently by a nineteeth century cook working in the Rutland Arms Hotel. Very fine Stilton cheese is made at the dairy in Hartington from the milk of Peakland cows.

Famous writers have penned the virtues of the Peak but none has better links than Izaak Walton, who fished The Dove with Charles Cotton.

Industry has always made its mark. Pack-horse, or 'jaggers' tracks can still be followed on foot over the northern moors. Saltways crossed the southern dales. Water-powered mills in the early part of the Industrial Revolution brought textile production to the dales. Fluorspar, a nuisance to the early lead miners, is now extracted by open-cast mining; it is used as a flux in steel making and as the basis for a number of chemicals.

Today, without any doubt, it is quarrying which makes the greatest industrial impact on the face of the Peak District. Limestone, suitable either as road aggregates or for cement making, is found only in scenically attractive areas and, as a result, the quarries can make an ugly scar on the landscape unless they are carefully monitored.

8 GEOLOGY

The rocks which form the foundations of the Peak District were laid down millions of years ago in a warm sea. Myriads of sea creatures living on the slimy bottom built up the great depth of limestone. Tropical lagoons were fringed by coral reefs which, through time, have become the rounded hills of Thorpe Cloud, Parkhouse, and Chrome Hills in Dove Dale. Minor volcanic activity took place during this time. The best examples of this can be found in the small outcrops of basalt near Castleton and in the dolerite quarry which is part of the Tideswell Dale Nature Trail. Lead found its way in gaseous form, through minute cracks in the underlying rocks, laying down the basis of what became a major industry thousands of centuries later. Copper was also deposited in this way, occurring beneath Ecton Hill in the Manifold valley.

A mighty river delta flooded into the tropical sea, depositing mud and sand which consolidated to make the gritstones of the Dark Peak and the shales of Mam Tor.

Gradually, the layers of limestone and gritstone bulged from pressures deep within the earth and the middle and edges split. Ice action later honed the land into the beginning of the Peak District's rocky pattern. At the end of the Ice Age, huge volumes of melt water continued this shaping. The water carved caverns within the limestone of Castleton

and Matlock as well as the pot holes of Eldon, and it also created the beautiful dales. The land tilted as it buckled to give west-facing gritstone outcrops on both sides of the Peak.

9 WILDLIFE IN THE PEAK

Grouse spend their hardy lives on the high moors of the Dark Peak feeding on the tender shoots of young heather. Their tough existence is rudely shattered for four months of every year beginning on the 'Glorious Twelfth of August'. Not so common, and regrettably often shot by mistake, are their cousins the black grouse. Birds of prey have their chosen areas, and many migrants, some quite rare, visit quieter sanctuaries on the moors from time to time. Mountain hares are common despite an inability quickly to shed their winter camouflage once the snows have gone. Foxes live a frugal life, mainly dependent upon voles and other small creatures. Plant life on the acid moors has to be tough to combat the extreme weather conditions. Heathers, coarse grass, and berry plants such as bilberry, cloudberry, and crowberry manage to survive in this harsh environment.

The limestone plateau is much more gentle. It is mainly given over to grazing, and masses of colourful flowers still fill the hayfields and road verges. Scabious, meadow cranesbill, and other plants, which were once scarce, have made a recent comeback in fields where far-sighted farmers have moved back to natural and cheaper methods of fertilizing the land. Plant, and to a certain extent, animal life, in the dales depend on the underlying strata. The Upper Derwent and its tributaries flow mostly through shale and gritstone. Forests planted around the Derwent Reservoirs are a major feature and offer homes to woodland birds and a few deer, as well as to, the smaller carnivorous animals. In the limestone dales, trees were once cut down for fuel but they are plentiful today and, in some instances, they are crowding other plant life. In Dove Dale, a courageous scheme has removed much of the invasive woodland to recreate more open vistas. Plant life on the craggy scree-covered hillsides is mostly dwarf and has an almost alpine quality. But the dales are best known for their trout streams. Not only do game fish breed in their clear waters, but the crayfish, a crustacean which needs pure water, is found beneath the rocks of most of the rivers in the dales.

Walk 1
LAD'S LEAP
6 miles (9½ km) Strenuous; one climb of 984 feet (300 m), NOT SUITABLE IN MIST OR BAD WEATHER

This moorland walk is along a rocky escarpment high above Manchester's water supply in the Longdendale Valley, an ideal introduction to the wild moors of the northern section of the Dark Peak. Taking advantage of newly created rights of access and well-defined footpaths, the walk climbs steeply above a series of reservoirs to reach the escarpment of Lad's Leap. This it does by way of an old track which served a long-abandoned gritstone quarry. From Lad's Leap, wide-ranging views can be enjoyed of Bleaklow and Kinder Scout to the south across Longdendale. Part of the Pennine Way National Trail is used on the descent. As parts of the route cover grouse moors which are closed for a few days each year during the shooting season, or during times of high fire risk, check the published lists issued by the Peak District National Park, either at information centres or on notices fastened to access gateways.

As with all moorland walks, consider local weather conditions before setting out.

The walk starts at the abandoned level crossing on the B6105 Glossop to Woodhead road. Parking for three or four cars is usually available to the west of the level crossing, or alternatively at the Torside car park a little over ½ mile (800 m) to the east.

A Longdendale Reservoirs from Torside Dam. Five reservoirs fill the valley bottom. They were constructed by Manchester Corporation between 1848 and 1878; for its time, the scheme was the largest artificial complex in Europe. The now-closed railway predates the reservoirs by only a year or so. When the first of the Woodhead tunnels at the dale head was built, at least thirty-two men died from accidents and cholera, and many others were injured. Eventually, three tunnels were built for this, the Manchester to Sheffield section of the Great Central Line. All are closed to traffic, but one now carries electricity transmission cables beneath the moors.

B Lad's Leap. Extensive views on all sides of this high vantage point take in most of the Dark Peak. The deep trough of Longdendale carves its way into the wild moors of the Woodhead Pass on your left. Directly ahead and on the far side of the dale, walkers on the Pennine Way use the ravine of Torside Clough to gain access to, or descend from, Bleaklow. Beyond it is the flat summit of Kinder Scout and, moving to the right, there are the subsidiary moors of Combs Moss and grassy ridges above Lyme Park marking the eastern limits of the Cheshire Plain. On a clear day you can pick out the telecommunication tower on Sutton Common (*see* Walk 33) about 20 miles (32 km) to the south-west, and occasionally the hills of North Wales. Closer to hand and still on your right, the Etherow drains from the lowest reservoir to wind its way beneath Werneth Low and join the River Mersey. Tintwistle Moors point the way to the urban sprawl of Greater Manchester.

C Looking to the left along Crowden Brook. The Pennine Way snakes towards Laddow Rocks, a traditional training ground for local climbers. Holme Moss television mast looms strangely above the forbidding moors on the far side of the valley. Below this viewpoint is the hamlet of Crowden where a row of quarry workers' cottages has been converted into a comfortable Youth Hostel; there is also a campsite, together with picnic facilities and a car park.

D Torside Reservoir is used by a sailing club. Watching races and general sailing activities can make an ideal finish to this walk.

Over

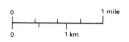

0   1 mile

0   1 km

6 *Climb a ladder stile and follow the moorland path in the direction of a signpost to Lad's Leap and Laddow.*

7 *On reaching the escarpment edge, turn right along a level, rocky path.*

8 *Keep to the left of the ruined wall and begin to descend along a cairned path, at first between banks of peat, then beside a wall.*

5 *Continue ahead beyond the old quarry, uphill along a rocky path.*

9 *At the small plantation, go to the right and climb a ladder stile. Follow the path gently downhill.*

4 *Go over the gateside stile next to a concessionary footpath sign. Follow the forest track upwards towards the boulder-strewn hillside.*

10 *Turn right at the junction, go along a cart track next to a pine wood, and carry on over the brow of the hill.*

3 *Cross the road diagonally left and go through a metal gate. Follow the track uphill. Bear right at a bridleway sign, and zig-zag uphill towards the plantation, ignoring two side tracks to the right.*

11 *Cross the main road and go through a gap in the wall opposite. Turn right, go down the steps, then through woodland to the right of the reservoir.*

2 *Turn right along the access road and cross the dam wall. Follow the road through trees to the main A628.*

1 *Go down the reservoir access road and turn left at a gate to follow a grassy track.*

12 *Turn left at the gate and go down a flight of steps to the access road. Follow it over the dam wall, then climb left to the B6105.*

Map labels: Pennine Way, Lad's Leap, 500, Tinwistle Knarr, Coombes Clough, Rhodeswood Reservoir, Valehouse Reservoir, Torside Reservoir, A 628 (T), Railway, B 6105, Dismantled, Glossop

B, C, D, A

Walk 2
MIDDLE MOOR AND LITTLE HAYFIELD
5 miles (8 km) Moderate

0   1 mile

0   1 km

This is a valley stroll combined with a moorland ramble which offers wide-ranging views of Kinder Scout and its satellite moors. Well-defined paths allow it to be used in all but the severest weather conditions. The walk starts from the ancient stone-built village of Hayfield now bypassed by the busy A624 and where ample parking can usually be found in the Sett Valley Trail car park.

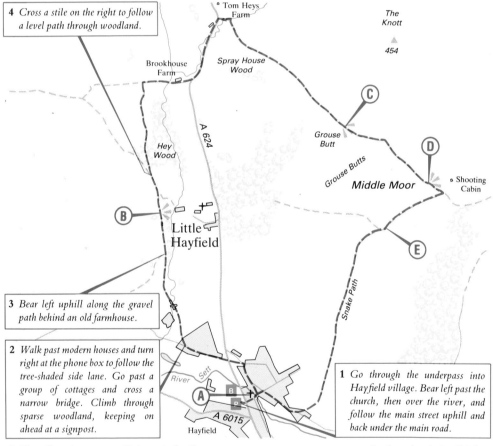

4 *Cross a stile on the right to follow a level path through woodland.*

Tom Heys Farm

The Knott

454

Brookhouse Farm

Spray House Wood

A 624

Hey Wood

Grouse Butt

Grouse Butts

Middle Moor

Shooting Cabin

C

D

B

Little Hayfield

E

Snake Path

3 *Bear left uphill along the gravel path behind an old farmhouse.*

2 *Walk past modern houses and turn right at the phone box to follow the tree-shaded side lane. Go past a group of cottages and cross a narrow bridge. Climb through sparse woodland, keeping on ahead at a signpost.*

River Sett

A   **B**   **D**

A 6015

Hayfield

1 *Go through the underpass into Hayfield village. Bear left past the church, then over the river, and follow the main street uphill and back under the main road.*

A Travellers have set off from Hayfield for centuries. Originally at the start of a pack-horse trail, it is now the hospitable venue for walkers climbing Kinder Scout.

B Look back at Hayfield in its sheltering hollow. Beyond it is Mount Famine and, to the right across the broad col, is Chinley Churn. To your left are the craggy ramparts of Kinder Scout.

Over

14

0   1 mile

0   1 km

5 *Turn right at the signpost and into a side valley. Turn right again along the surfaced lane as far as the main road. Turn left for about ¼ mile (400 m). Because there is no path take care as you go along the road, remembering to face the oncoming traffic.*

6 *Opposite the group of cottages, turn right at the gate. Bear right to a footbridge, cross, and climb the winding moorland path.*

7 *Turn right at the signpost to 'Hayfield' and walk along a sandy path meandering across the heather moor.*

Tom Heys Farm

The Knott

▲ 454

Brookhouse Farm

Spray House Wood

C

Hey Wood

A624

Grouse Butt

Grouse Butts

D

Middle Moor

Shooting Cabin

B

Little Hayfield

E

Snake Path

Hayfield

9 *Go down a flight of steps and turn right along the road into Hayfield. The car park and bus terminus are beyond the underpass behind the church.*

A 6015

A   B

8 *Go through a kissing gate and, after 100 yards (90 m), bear left on a descending path.*

C Ahead, Kinder Scout fills the far skyline, and to its right is the whaleback of Kinder Low; then Brown Knoll's long ridge leads to the twin summits of South Head and Mount Famine. Look right again to Chinley Churn and the low rolling hills above the Sett Valley.

D The tiny cabin to your left is used by grouse shooters during the season. Beyond is the western escarpment of Kinder Scout.

E The path on the left leads across the shoulder of Kinder to the Snake Pass.

15

Walk 3

LANTERN PIKE

4¼ miles (7 km) Easy/Moderate

Here is a gentle high-level walk, mostly using field paths around the shapely mass of Lantern Pike, an outlier of the central heights of the Dark Peak. Offering wide-ranging views to the north, south-west, and east, the moorland hilltop is a National Trust property which was bought by the Manchester Ramblers Federation in 1949 as a memorial to Edwin Royce one of their past presidents.

The walk starts from the Little Mill Inn near the scattered moorland hamlet of Rowarth. To reach it, drive north for about 2 miles (3¼ km) along an unclassified road from New Mills as far as a crossroads, then follow signposts into Rowarth. Alternatively, take the Mellor road east from the A626 at Marple Bridge to the crossroads and turn left.

There is a small car park near the road end but, if it is full, try to park where you will not block access to someone's driveway or the entrance to a farmer's field.

A Aspenshaw Hall is on your left, an attractive small Victorian mansion set in mature woodland with clumps of rhododendrons which grow well in the local acidic soil.

B The small industrial town of New Mills sits below and to your right on either side of a ravine where the River Sett forces its way, once powering the mills which gave the town its name. Below the town centre, the Sett joins the River Goyt, a river which drains moors further south.

On the furthest right skyline a solitary tower called Lyme Cage was used by the ladies of Lyme Hall in times gone by to watch the chase in the nearby deerpark. Turn left and the rolling moorland across the valley opposite is Chinley Churn; then turn left again for the brooding mass of Kinder Scout.

C Pause to enjoy the fine views of Kinder Scout and the village of Hayfield, framed by tree branches as you climb the farm lane.

D Lantern Pike is above and to your left. A National Trust property, it can be climbed by following the skyline ridge across the summit and rejoining the main footpath further on. A plaque on the summit indicates the positions of numerous features which can be seen from this point.

E Cown Edge is ahead and beyond it the vast rugged moors of aptly named Bleaklow. Cown Edge is the focal point of a waymarked route from Hazel Grove near Stockport to Gee Cross on the A560 near Hyde.

Over

0   1 mile
0   1 km

2 *Do not use the farm lane, but continue ahead over a stile and follow a grassy path towards, then below, a belt of trees.*

1 *Walk along the lane past the Little Mill Inn for about 200 yards (180 m). Then turn right at a signpost to cross three fields to a farm.*

8 *At the junction of six tracks, climb the stone stile diagonally opposite and follow the direction of a fingerpost. There is no path so keep to the left of the shallow valley and walk round the hillside, using stiles and gates to follow the route.*

9 *Go to the left through the farmyard, then right downhill along the lane. Follow it to Rowarth.*

Rowarth

Bullshaw
Farm

P

Long Lee
Farm

Blackshaw
Farm

Laneside
Farm

Thornsett Fields
Farm

E

*Lantern
Pike*
▲
373

Aspenshaw
Hall

D

*Sunny
Side*

Upper Cliffe
Farm

A

Wethercotes

B

C

3 *Turn left uphill along the lane, then keep straight ahead at the track above Feeding Hey Farm.*

7 *Continue on by footpath at the lane-end.*

River   Sett

4 *Turn right at the junction, going gently downhill along a cart track.*

5 *Turn left downhill along the road for ¼ mile (400 m).*

6 *Turn left at the end of a row of cottages to climb a farm track. Continue ahead at the junction.*

Walk 4
KINDER DOWNFALL
8 miles (13 km) Strenuous; one climb of 1247 feet (380 m), boggy stretches, NOT SUITABLE IN MIST OR BAD WEATHER

This classic route is not a walk for the ill-prepared, be he or she improperly clothed for the prevailing weather conditions at 2000 feet (600 m), or generally unfit for what is an expedition across an open mountainside on the same latitude as Siberia. Remember that a warm sunny day in Hayfield can frequently turn to arctic style weather on Kinder. Having given that warning, walkers who act sensibly will enjoy this exhilarating high-level walk through some of the most rugged countryside in the Peak District. The sense of achievement on looking back at the wild rocks around the Downfall will be just reward for the effort of the climb.

As you climb William's Clough and turn towards the summit, spare a thought for those people who fought valiantly for the freedom to roam the wild open moors of the Peak District and were not afraid of imprisonment for their beliefs.

The walk starts from Bowden Bridge car park on the Kinder road from Hayfield. Leave the A624 and drive into the centre of the village; then follow a side road (Kinder Road) eastwards. If the car park is full, there is usually space along the road in the direction of Hayfield. Do not drive beyond Bowden Bridge as parking is restricted upstream of this point. Hayfield is served by several bus routes.

A A plaque on the quarry wall above the car park at Bowden Bridge commemorates the Mass Trespass on 24 April 1932 which led to five protesters being jailed for between two and six months. It has been argued that the trespass was unnecessary, but it and others which followed, certainly functioned as the catalyst which brought about post-war legislation to create National Parks and allow a greater freedom of access to the lonely places of England and Wales.

B Kinder Reservoir, one of Stockport's water supplies, is below. Two streams feed it from the east, the main one being the River Kinder which drains the boggy plateau of Kinder Scout. The other is William's Clough, named after a blacksmith whose now drowned smithy once stood at the bottom of this steep valley. His trade was mostly repairing the shoes of pack-ponies climb-ing the track over to the Snake Pass. At one time, this path was the only right of way to the north of Kinder.

C Look down the rocky gorge towards the reservoir, and to the right of the stream there is a small pool where a mermaid is supposed to live. If you want to see her, come to the pool on a summer's night and, if you are lucky, you will be entertained by her charms, but beware as many have disappeared after a night by the Mermaid's Pool!

One of the possible origins of the title Kinder Scout, is from the Saxon *kyndwr scut* meaning 'water over the edge'. In summer an almost insignificant trickle flows over the steep jumble of crags known as the Downfall but, after heavy rain and with a strong westerly wind, a plume of water blows backwards and can be seen for miles. The crags are a popular climbing face, both for rock-climbers in summer and for devotees of ice climbing in winter. During particularly harsh winters, the ravine and surrounding rocks take on the appearance of a glacier.

D A $\frac{1}{4}$ mile (400 m) diversion upstream from the Downfall along the sandy bed of the River Kinder leads to the twin outcropping crags of Kinder Gate Stones. The Pennine Way route crosses Kinder at this point and many ambitions of prospective 'Wayfarers' have foundered on the first day. Above and on all sides of the river, the boggy plateau of Kinder Scout waits to sap the strength of ill-prepared walkers. Deep, water-worn channels known as 'groughs' can lead the unwary astray.

Return to the Downfall to continue the walk along, then below, the western escarpment.

Over

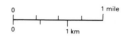

0   1 mile

0   1 km

4 *Turn right along a path contouring to the left of the reservoir.*

5 *Go down to the stream, turn left, and follow it uphill, crossing as indicated by the steep path.*

6 *Turn right on the broad moorland saddle. Climb steeply up to the escarpment.*

A624

Mill Hill

544

7 *Follow the path to the right around the rocky edge.*

3 *Turn left and go downhill across the valley. Turn right and go uphill along a rocky path above the reservoir buildings.*

Leygatehead Moor

William Clough

8 *Cross the rocky stream bed and begin to go downhill along the moorland path.*

Ⓑ

600

Ⓒ Ⓓ

Kinder Downfall

2 *Turn right, cross the bridge, and follow the lane uphill past the farm.*

Kinder Reservoir

Cluther Rocks

Kinder Scout

629

Hayfield

Ⓐ

Kinder Road

Bowden Bridge

P

The Three Knolls

Kinder Low

Tunstead Clough Farm

9 *Turn sharp right and cross a stream. Go to the right again across a depression and follow the path steeply downhill.*

1 *Follow the reservoir road uphill from the car park.*

10 *Go ahead at the path crossing to follow a wall downhill towards a stile. Cross and continue to descend through improving farmland. Use kissing gates and stiles as necessary.*

11 *Keep to the left of the house, then follow the waymarked path to the right, around the farm buildings. Join the access track and follow it downhill into the valley.*

12 *Turn right along the valley-bottom road; follow it back to the car park.*

Walk 5

SOUTH HEAD

$4\frac{1}{2}$ miles ($7\frac{1}{4}$ km) Moderate; muddy sections

This walk follows bridleways and ancient pack-horse trails around the shapely summit of South Head. As most of the tracks are walled, they make this high-level walk safe to follow in all but the most inclement weather conditions.

Limited roadside parking can usually be found along lanes leading away from the settlement surrounding the Crown and Mitre Inn at New Smithy near Chinley. The hamlet is on the A624, Chapel-en-le-Frith to Glossop road immediately north of the railway bridge.

A At the top of the first rise there is a 'surprise view' ahead towards the sharp peak of South Head, the crux of this walk. To its left can be seen the more rounded outline of Mount Famine. Left again across the valley is rugged Cracken Edge, the quarried eastern escarpment of Chinley Churn. Looking down the valley, we see the outskirts of Chinley and New Mills, dominated to their left by the attractive summit of Eccles Pike. Further left again and almost completing the circle is the flat top of Combs Moss.

B Pause at the top of the climb and look back towards the broad headwaters of the Goyt Valley. To their left is Combs Moss, and moving right are the heather moors surrounding the Cat and Fiddle Inn at the highest point of the A537, Buxton to Macclesfield Road. Shining Tor, the highest point on the far horizon, points to a long western ridge above the Goyt Valley.

C Here, you are looking across the upper section of the Sett Valley to lands owned by the National Trust. On the far side of the depression, the massive bulk of Kinder Low reaches towards the sky, and beyond it are the craggy north-western ramparts of Kinder Scout itself pointing the way to William's Clough, once one of only two authorized ways around the western side of the Kinder moors. The other is the track which you can probably see rising from grassy fields in the valley beneath your feet and climbing to the right-hand edge of Kinder Low.

D Look south into the northern limits of the White Peak. A dominant plume of white smoke in the middle distance is from limeworks and roadstone quarries surrounding Buxton. The contrast between the topography of the White and Dark Peaks is noticeable from here; in the south, or White Peak, the lime-stone uplands are flat and carved with deep valleys which are hidden from view at this point. The Dark Peak by contrast is more rugged. Cattle graze the sweet, lush, upland pastures of the White Peak, but they are restricted to the valleys of the Dark Peak, and only limited numbers of sheep can find sustenance on the poor grasses of the lower moors. Grouse are the only commercially viable inhabitants of the heather moors.

E This view is across the upper section of the Black Brook valley towards the town of Chapel-en-le-Frith, the self-styled capital of the Peak District. As the name suggests, the town developed around a simple foresters' chapel in the frith or Royal Forest of the Peak. In this case, the forest was a royal hunting preserve. The town fits snugly in a hollow beneath Combs Moss, and many of its inhabitants are employed by the Ferodo Company whose main factory is on the near outskirts of the town. Ferodo make brake and clutch linings, an industry which began when the founder noticed that carters improved the efficiency of their brakes by wedging a clog or shoe between the brake block and the cart's wheels when descending the steep Peakland hills.

Over

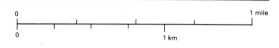

0   1 mile

0
1 km

4 At a complex of track junctions, go through the third gate on your right to walk along a rough cart track. Where the track turns sharp left over a stream, continue ahead and cross a stile next to a narrow gate. Climb steeply up the part-walled grassy path.

5 At the top of the slope, go over a stile and turn right. Go through a gate to follow the path across a broad, grassy saddle and around the shoulder of South Head.

6 Continue ahead at the footpath sign, through a small notch in the hillside, then downhill along a walled stony track.

7 Where the track widens, go through the right-hand of a pair of gates, downhill along a field track above the deep, partly wooded valley.

South Head 494

Ⓒ

Ⓑ

Ⓓ

Andrews Farm

A 624

3 Go left at the farm down to, and across, a little stream. Turn right and climb the walled muddy path to the next farm. Follow its access lane until it turns left, then continue ahead along a walled grassy track. Go to the right at the third farm and follow a cart track away.

Bennett Barn

Ⓔ

Shireoaks

Ⓐ

8 Bear right at the farmyard and out along its access track, at first downhill then more level.

B 6062

Hull End

New Smithy

Gorsty Low

Breckhead

9 Walk past a cluster of farm cottages and turn right along the road for 100 yards (90 m). Turn left at the right-hand of a pair of gates and go to the right and around the back of a large house. Go through a gate and turn right along a field path. Follow the boundary wall downhill. Go over a stile and along a narrow path to reach the side road. The inn and main road are to your left.

2 Turn left at the 'No Through Road' sign and follow the walled farm lane uphill.

1 Follow the winding lane to the left of the Crown and Mitre Inn.

Walk 6

CHINLEY CHURN

4¼ miles (7 km) Moderate; one steady climb of 774 feet (238 m)

Walled lanes lead to a high open moor where the views cover the Cheshire uplands as well as the dramatic outline of Kinder Scout. Easy footpaths lead downhill to make this a safe walk. Park in the layby opposite the converted Zion chapel on the A6015 in Birch Vale.

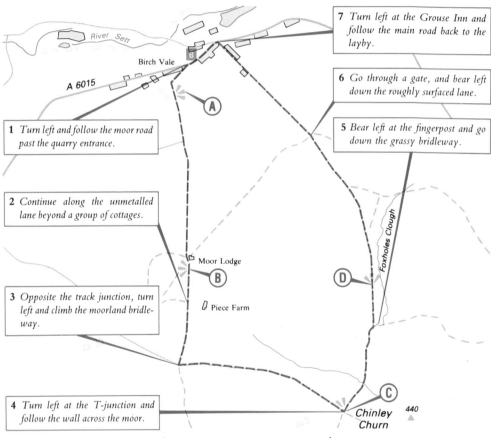

7 *Turn left at the Grouse Inn and follow the main road back to the layby.*

6 *Go through a gate, and bear left down the roughly surfaced lane.*

5 *Bear left at the fingerpost and go down the grassy bridleway.*

1 *Turn left and follow the moor road past the quarry entrance.*

2 *Continue along the unmetalled lane beyond a group of cottages.*

3 *Opposite the track junction, turn left and climb the moorland bridleway.*

4 *Turn left at the T-junction and follow the wall across the moor.*

River Sett

Birch Vale

A 6015

Moor Lodge

Piece Farm

Foxholes Clough

Chinley Churn 440

A Birch Vale quarry is on the left. Do not enter it but, from the gateway, look towards the quarry face. The Dark Peak's bedrocks are layered below a sparse topsoil.

B Looking west, the Cheshire Plain spreads itself beyond the Sett Valley.

C Greater Manchester is to the north-west and, on a clear day, you can see Winter Hill above Bolton.

D The wooded middle section of the River Sett is below. To the right is Kinder with the path climbing William's Clough on its left. Vehicles climbing the A624 across Hollingworth Head point the way to Bleaklow's moors.

22

LANGSETT

$3\frac{3}{4}$ **miles (6 km) Easy**

Here is an ideal moorland walk for a hot summer's day. A major part of the route enjoys the shade of pine trees lining the banks of Langsett Reservoir, and easy-to-follow paths keep the reservoir in sight at all times. The walk starts and finishes at the picnic site and car park at the side of the A616 Manchester to Sheffield road on the outskirts of Langsett village. The Waggon and Horses Inn is only a short distance away and makes an ideal venue for the end of the walk.

3 *Go through a wide gap in the old stone wall on your left, then gradually downhill along a moorland path.*

2 *Turn left at the path junction, downhill along a stony track. Cross the stone-arched bridge and bear left. Climb a zig-zag path to reach the open moor beyond the forest edge.*

1 *Follow the woodland path to the right, away from the car park.*

7 *Turn left at the road junction, downhill and across the dam wall. Turn left at the main road, past the Waggon and Horses inn to reach the car park.*

B Crookland Wood

A 616(T)

Langsett

A

Langsett Bank

C

Langsett Reservoir

D

North America

Highcliff Common

Mauk Royd

Nab

Upper Midhope

Thickwood

4 *Continue ahead at the ruined farm house and along a path marked 'Privilege Footpath'.*

5 *Go through a metal gate to follow a track between two sections of pine forest.*

6 *Continue ahead along the concrete access lane and ahead again on reaching the road.*

A The barn next to the car park is one of the largest of its kind in the Peak District. Abandoned for years, it is being converted into a National Park Information Centre, and Ranger Briefing and Community Centre. The syllable 'sett' indicates that Langsett was once the site of a Nordic farmstead or *saetre*.

B Fir trees frame this attractive view of Langsett Reservoir.

C Look uphill to the right towards the Derwent Moors.

The path you have just left was originally used by pack-horses; it crosses a broad col known as Cut Gate to the right of the skyline.

D The peat-stained waters of the reservoir have drained from Harden and Midhope Moors.

LOSE HILL

5 miles (8 km) Moderate/Strenuous; one climb of 905 feet (276 m)

Lose Hill is the eastern end of a long ridge on the north side of the Hope Valley. Castleton, where the walk starts and finishes, is a popular village with many amenities, ranging from its four tourist caves to the ancient grandeur of its Norman castle. The walk is along the broad, airy ridge where the wide-ranging views encompass most of the Dark Peak.

There is ample car parking at the side of the A625 in Castleton village. A regular bus service links it with Sheffield, and there is a railway station nearby at Hope.

A The village of Castleton still sits under the benign protection of a castle founded in 1080 by William Peveril. Built to control lead-mining activity in the area, an industry which continued from Roman times until the present century, the castle led a peaceful life. Its only highlight was in 1157 when Henry II accepted the submission of Malcolm, King of Scotland, within its walls.

Although the parish church of St Edmund was substantially rebuilt in the last century, it has Norman foundations. Inside, it has a fine Norman chancel arch, seventeenth-century box pews, and a collection of venerable books including a Breeches Bible dating from 1611.

On 29 May every year, the village celebrates a curious festival, the Garland Ceremony. The focal point is a man dressed in Jacobean costume and accompanied by a similarly dressed consort. He rides through the village with his head and trunk covered by a huge cone, or 'garland' of flowers. Officially commemorating the Restoration of the Monarchy in 1660, the ceremony is doubtless pagan in origin.

An old shop in the street leading to the castle has been converted into a National Park Information Centre. Old lead mining implements and a small exhibition describing the local countryside complete this tiny, yet imaginative, centre.

Show caves vie for the attention of the visitor to Castleton. The most natural is Peak Cavern, a wide opening beneath a dramatic cliff topped by the castle. The others are partly natural, partly abandoned lead mines. Speedwell Cavern, at the foot of the Winnats Pass, is visited by boat, and Treak Cliff, across the hillside to the north-west, has some beautiful stalagmites and stalactites. Blue John Mine further round the same hillside is probably the deepest.

B At Hollins Cross, pause at the top of the climb and look back towards Castleton. The chasm of Peak's Hole and the cavern are to the right of the castle; then look right again to the Winnats Pass, once a wave-washed opening in a coral reef.

Continue looking right across Treak Cliff to Mam Tor, where its loose, shaly east face at the head of the Hope Valley suggests its local name, the 'Shivering Mountain'. Land at its foot has slipped so badly that, after many years spent trying to keep it in repair, the A625 has been abandoned by the county roads authority. There is an Iron Age fort on the summit. To the north of this viewpoint is the Edale Valley, and beyond it stands the massive bulk of Kinder Scout.

C Take care not to go too close to the shaly edge of Back Tor, especially in wet or windy weather.

D The hilltop of Lose Hill was donated to the National Trust in memory of G H B Ward who furthered the cause of access to the open moors. This is one of the finest viewpoints in the Peak and a plaque indicates most of the distant features.

E The Victorian mansion of Lose Hill Hall is now a Peak District National Park Study Centre. Courses are held to create a greater awareness of the countryside, and range from walking and activity holidays to craft instruction and environmental studies.

Over

0 _____ 1 mile

0 _____ 1 km

3 *Turn right at the viewpoint indicator and follow the ridge-top path.*

4 *Go to the left across a stile, then immediately right and climb shaly Back Tor. Continue along the ridge towards Lose Hill.*

5 *Go to the right, downhill and over a stile. Begin to bear right again beyond a prominent cairn, then left to pass a line of trees.*

6 *Turn right at a signpost to Castleton and cross the stile by a second, to go downhill across fields as indicated by yellow waymarks.*

7 *Do not go into the farmyard, but turn left to cross a stile and follow a path around the edge of the field above a shallow brook:*

8 *Turn right along the lane and left at the junction. Go down to the road and turn right to reach the centre of the village.*

2 *At a signpost, continue ahead and away from the lane, uphill along a sunken path. Cross a stile and slant left up the open hillside.*

1 *Walk along the main street past the shops and the school. Go down the narrow side lane and follow it towards the ridge.*

Map labels:

D

476
Tumulus
Lose Hill

Back
Tor

Backtor
Nook

Brockett Booth
Plantation

Round
Plantation

Hollins
Cross
B

C

Barker Bank

Losehill
Farm

Mam
Plantation

Only Grange
Farm

Riding House
Farm

Field's
Farm

Lose Hill
Hall

E

Caravan Site

A 625

Castleton

P

i

A

25

HALLAM MOORS

4¼ miles (7 km) Easy

Easy moorland footpaths link Redmires Reservoir with woodlands of the Rivelin Valley. The return is by way of Wyming Brook where the tranquil views are in marked contrast with the bustle of Sheffield's city centre barely 5 miles (8 km) away.

Park at the head of Wyming Brook about a mile (1½ km) west of Lodge Moor hospital which is served by buses.

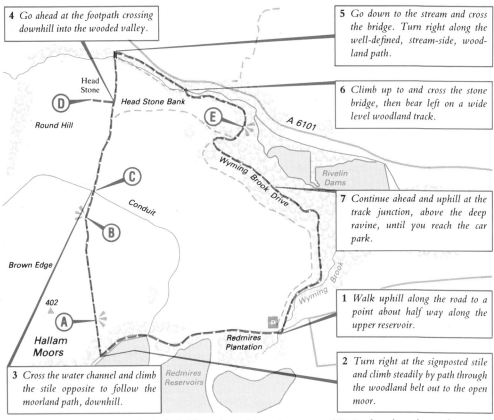

4 Go ahead at the footpath crossing downhill into the wooded valley.

5 Go down to the stream and cross the bridge. Turn right along the well-defined, stream-side, woodland path.

6 Climb up to and cross the stone bridge, then bear left on a wide level woodland track.

7 Continue ahead and uphill at the track junction, above the deep ravine, until you reach the car park.

1 Walk uphill along the road to a point about half way along the upper reservoir.

2 Turn right at the signposted stile and climb steadily by path through the woodland belt out to the open moor.

3 Cross the water channel and climb the stile opposite to follow the moorland path, downhill.

(Map labels: Head Stone; Head Stone Bank; Round Hill; Conduit; Brown Edge; 402; Hallam Moors; A 6101; Wyming Brook Drive; Rivelin Dams; Wyming Brook; Redmires Plantation; Redmires Reservoirs)

A From here, you can look across Redmires Reservoir towards Sheffield.

B Rivelin Valley points the way to the Derwent Moors. Gritstone outcrops, features of the high moors, dot the skyline.

C The channel carries water from the north side of the moor to Redmires Reservoir.

D A little off-route to the left of the path, the aptly named Head Stone probably held religious significance in prehistoric times.

E Leafy branches frame a delightful view of the Rivelin Dams below in their densely wooded setting.

26

Walk 10

WIN HILL

$5\frac{1}{4}$ miles ($8\frac{1}{2}$ km) Strenuous; one climb of 958 feet (292 m), NOT RECOMMENDED IN MIST

A steep climb from lush farmland is rewarded by a long heather-covered ridgewalk with a fine viewpoint over much of the Peak District.

There is a small official car park in the centre of Hope village but, if it is full, you can usually find space along the Edale road. Please park without

inconveniencing other road users. Sheffield buses serve Hope, and there is a railway station nearby.

9 *Turn left on joining the sunken track.*

8 *Almost at the forest wall, go through an old gateway and turn left downhill.*

7. *Walk ahead along a wide sandy track across the broad heather ridge. Ignore any side paths.*

6 *Enter the forest and turn left on a path climbing towards the open moor. Climb steeply to the summit.*

10 *Go through the farmyard then follow waymarks out to the open fields. Continue by path.*

Win Hill

5 *Bear left at a junction and walk along a wide, level, grassy path towards the pine forest.*

11 *Follow the lane away from a modern house. Go under the railway, then over the bridge, and turn left along the Edale road.*

4 *Turn left at the signpost to Ladybower, going uphill along the narrow lane leading to a steeply climbing field path.*

1 *Take the Edale road for about $\frac{1}{4}$ mile (400 m); turn right along a side lane, down to, and over, a bridge, then right again along an unsurfaced riverside track. Keep to the right at the house, then turn left and go over a stile to follow a field path, diagonally right.*

2 *Turn left uphill, go under the railway bridge, and bear right towards the farm. Turn right along its access lane.*

3 *Turn left uphill by a road through the scattered hamlet. Ignore a signpost to Win Hill.*

A The riverside house was once a water-powered textile mill; its wheel now stands above the riverbank.

B Looking along the Hope Valley towards Mam Tor, this view is marred only by the chimney of the Hope Valley cement works.

C From the summit of Win Hill a heather ridge points towards Lose Hill opposite. Beyond it, a long curving ridge marks the south side of Edale and, to the right, Kinder Scout bulks huge, separated from Bleaklow by the trough of the Snake Pass. To the right is the Derwent Valley

topped by a line of weirdly shaped gritstone outcrops.

D Lose Hill's conical shape is most evident from here. Traditionally, it is where a battle was lost and another won on Win Hill.

27

BRETTON CLOUGH

5 miles (8 km) Easy/Moderate

Starting from a friendly pub, The Barrel in the hamlet of Bretton high on Eyam Edge, the walk enjoys delightful views over the countryside surrounding the unspoilt wooded valley of Bretton Clough. By tradition, Bretton is the place where the last true Britons lived. There is no factual evidence to support this legend, but there was a Roman camp nearby at *Navio* between Hope and Bradwell. Using it as a base, the Romans collected slaves from the surrounding population to work in nearby lead mines, and possibly Bretton was a place where local tribes found sanctuary.

Roadside parking can be found uphill of The Barrel Inn. To reach it, take the minor road from Eyam and climb on to Eyam Edge; (Eyam is on the B6521 which leaves the A623 above Stoney Middleton). Alternatively, approach Bretton from Great Hucklow (side road between the A623 and B6049).

A The view covers most of the northern portion of the White Peak. Tiny villages sit below amid a complex pattern of stone walls enclosing ancient fields.

Gliders from the club on nearby Hucklow Edge soar on thermals rising from dales surrounding the Hope Valley. Mam Tor marks the upper limits of the valley, and its long ridge is the start of the Dark Peak. To the north lies Kinder Scout and the wild rolling moors of Bleaklow and the Derwent Edges.

B Bretton Clough points the way towards Hathersage, once the home of Little John, Robin Hood's right-hand man, who is buried in Hathersage churchyard. The long gritstone ridge of Stanage Edge marks the far skyline.

C Bretton Clough is too steep to farm. The scrubland is natural and favoured by a wide range of birdlife.

D The purpose-built Youth Hostel on the right could make an ideal family base in this part of the Peak District.

Over

0   1 mile
0   1 km

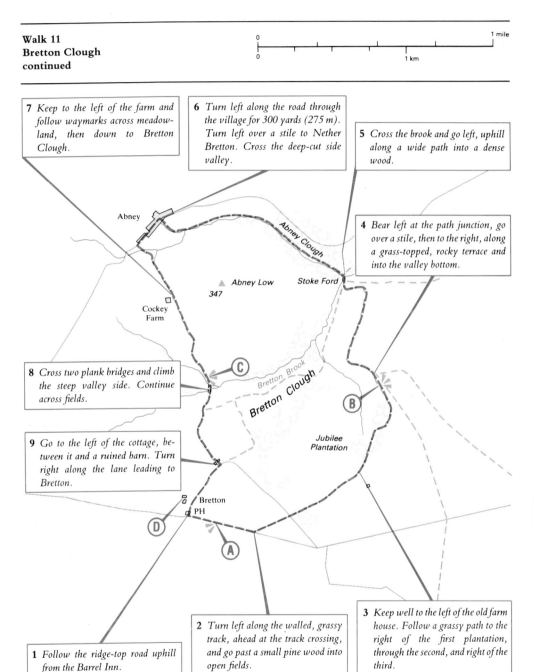

7 Keep to the left of the farm and follow waymarks across meadowland, then down to Bretton Clough.

6 Turn left along the road through the village for 300 yards (275 m). Turn left over a stile to Nether Bretton. Cross the deep-cut side valley.

5 Cross the brook and go left, uphill along a wide path into a dense wood.

Abney

Abney Clough

4 Bear left at the path junction, go over a stile, then to the right, along a grass-topped, rocky terrace and into the valley bottom.

▲ Abney Low
347   Stoke Ford

Cockey
Farm

8 Cross two plank bridges and climb the steep valley side. Continue across fields.

Ⓒ

Bretton Brook

Bretton Clough

Ⓑ

Jubilee
Plantation

9 Go to the left of the cottage, between it and a ruined barn. Turn right along the lane leading to Bretton.

Bretton
PH

Ⓓ

Ⓐ

3 Keep well to the left of the old farm house. Follow a grassy path to the right of the first plantation, through the second, and right of the third.

2 Turn left along the walled, grassy track, ahead at the track crossing, and go past a small pine wood into open fields.

1 Follow the ridge-top road uphill from the Barrel Inn.

29

Walk 12

CAVE DALE

$2\frac{1}{2}$ miles (4 km) Moderate; one climb of 656 feet (200 m)

The steep initial climb above the delightfully named Goosehill gives quick access to the limestone moors above Castleton, a means of escaping rapidly the crowds during busy periods.

Returning by dramatic and narrow Cave Dale, the walk is full of interest and may be combined with Walk 10 to give a full day's expedition.

There are two large car parks in Castleton and limited roadside spaces.

Castleton has several pubs and cafés together with shops and four show caves.

2 *Go through a metal gate and, after a few yards, begin to climb steeply to your left. Bear left on reaching a grassy terrace. Move to the right as you approach the lip of Cave Dale.*

1 *From the village square, follow the street on the left of the Youth Hostel. Cross the bridge and go half-left, uphill past old cottages.*

Goosehill

A 625

Town Ditch

Speedwell Cavern

Goosehill Hall

Peak Cavern

276

Peveril Castle (rems of)

Long Cliff

Cave Dale

3 *Go through a stile and bear left as indicated by the sign to Old Moor. Follow a grassy path.*

Cow Low

Mines (dis)

Mines (dis)

4 *Turn sharp left at the footpath junction, going downhill in to the narrow dale.*

5 *Go down the rocky, then grassy, dale-bottom path. Go through a bridlegate into Bargate. Turn left for the village square.*

A A narrow stream-side path on the left leads past an interesting group of old cottages to Peak cavern. The remains of a rope-walk can still be seen in the cavern entrance. Band concerts are occasionally held in this natural auditorium.

B Look across to the castle and on to the rooftops of the oldest part of Castleton.

C Look towards the Winnats, Treak Cliff, and Mam Tor's shaly east face. The Winnats or 'Wind Gates' were once part of a pack-horse route where, in 1758, a young couple eloping to Peak Forest were murdered.

D Lines of grassy hollows on the dale side are trial holes made by lead miners.

E Notice the small outcrop of hexagonal blocks of volcanic dolerite near the kissing gate.

F Peveril Castle sits proudly above the dale. Once used as a prison for miners breaking local laws, it was never involved in warfare.

Walk 13
FOOLOW AND SILLY DALE
3 miles (5 km) Easy

0   1 mile
0   1 km

There are no records of any simpleton either in Foolow or in Silly Dale. Foolow means a multi-coloured hill, possibly a refer ence to nearby Eyam Edge. Silly is Old English for pretty or happy, an apt description of this little-known dale.

The walk starts from Foolow village green where there is usually ample roadside parking. There is one pub.

4 *At the far side of a line of trees, turn left over a stile and follow arrows and paintmarks into Grindlow village.*

3 *Turn left along the narrow lane as far as the road, then left again.*

5 *Bear left along the village road then fork right towards the main road.*

2 *Turn left over a stone stile and follow the wall-side path.*

Hucklow Edge

Mine (dis)

Great Hucklow   Rose Farm
     Grindlow
Hall Farm

Ⓒ

Ⓑ

1 *Follow the Bretton Edge road northwards away from the village.*

6 *Cross the main road and go to the left of the bungalow, down a narrow, walled track.*

Ⓐ   W
Roods Farm   Foolow

Manor Farm

Ⓓ   Little Moor
Silly Dale
▲ 295

Old Hall Farm

Ⓔ

7 *Turn left at the T-junction and cross the dry dale. Turn left again over a stile, and bear right then half left uphill to follow a line of stiles across fields.*

8 *Follow the narrow alleyway past farm buildings and out on to the village green.*

A The well at the side of the road is protected by a wall with a narrow stile to keep animals away from the village's former supply of drinking water, once a scarcity on these dry limestone uplands. Regrettably the water is now unfit for human consumption.

B Gliders can usually be seen from the club high above Bretton Edge.

C Tree-screened hollows and rough ground uphill of this point indicate the position of abandoned lead-mining activity.

D Surface water has not flowed down Silly Dale for at least 10 000 years, when catastrophic floods marked the end of the last Ice Age. Flowers growing in the dale bottom include the white meadow saxifrage, purple cranesbill, and spotted orchids.

E Foolow is built around a wide village green with a duck-pond backed by a fourteenth-century cross and bull-ring stone.

31

Walk 14

CRESSBROOK DALE

6 miles (9½ km) Easy/Moderate

The walk explores and compares the scenery of the uplands and wooded dales around Cressbrook, a dale which is so special that it has been designated a nature reserve. Many interesting fossils can be found and admired in the limestone rocks along with the flowers of Cressbrook Dale. Links with the now abandoned industries of the area can be seen. On the higher ground, chert – a particularly hard form of limestone used in pottery making – was quarried below Longstone Edge. Water-powered and elegant Georgian Cressbrook Mill in the dale bottom was founded by Richard Arkwright and was one of the earliest textile mills in the area.

Parking is available at the Monsal Head scenic car park, or behind the Monsal Head Hotel.

A Rough ground at the left-hand side of the track indicates the site of an abandoned chert quarry. Chert is similar to the flint which occurs in the south of England, and both materials were used in the production of bone china.

B Heather is colonizing the moor on the right, a rarity on the limestone uplands of the White Peak. Humps and hollows to your left are the remains of trial holes and small pits left by lead miners.

C Half-right and in the middle distance, Eyam Edge marks the start of the Dark Peak. Kinder Scout, the highest point of Derbyshire can be seen beyond the plume of smoke issuing from the Hope Valley cement works. Closer to hand is the linear village of Wardlow, a feature of the White Peak where farms using a common water supply are infilled by attractive stone cottages.

D Cressbrook Dale is below, as pretty as its name suggests. Designated as a National Nature Reserve, many rare and semi-alpine plants bloom on its dry, grassy heights or in the shady woodland depths. Lily-of-the-valley, primroses, orchids, cowslips, and wood anemones can be found in spring and early summer. **Please do not pick any flowers because not only will it spoil the enjoyment of others, but will probably kill the parent plant.**

A cave in Ravencliffe, high on the left along the lip of the dale, once yielded gold objects left by the earliest people to live in the Peak District. **Please note that there is no public access to the cave.**

E Cressbrook Mill, a former textile mill, dates from 1815, and replaced one built in 1779 by Richard Arkwright. Water-cum-Jolly Dale, upstream of the mill, provided its water power. The elegant mill, which now shows signs of neglect, is topped by an interesting cupola. Orphans brought from London to work in the mill, were housed in the Gothic-like, lancet-windowed Apprentice House above the mill race.

F Monsal Trail. The walkers' and cyclists' route, the Monsal Trail, follows part of the old Midland Railway from Bakewell to Miller's Dale. The line, built at the height of the railway boom of the mid-nineteenth century, was planned to connect London and Manchester by following the Derwent Valley north from Derby. The intended route was along the valley as far as Hathersage where it would join the Sheffield to Manchester line. When it reached Rowsley, the then Duke of Devonshire realized the implications, and forbad progress through Chatsworth. For several years, the line finished at Rowsley before the Monsal line could be built.

The Peak Rail Society have plans to rebuild the line along Monsal Dale but, as yet, only short stretches from Buxton and Matlock are open.

G At Monsal Head the dale makes an almost right-angled turn beneath the viaduct. On your left is a group of rocks, called Hob House, which was once part of a coral reef. Prehistoric people lived at Fin Cop on the dale's rim high above the outcrop. (**No public access**).

Over

0 _____ 1 mile

0 _____
                1 km

9 Go past a group of cottages and turn left along the road. Then turn left along the valley road again on reaching the mill.

8 Climb the stile and bear left down the narrow path into the wooded dale.

7 Turn left along a walled grassy path marked to Ravendale.

6 Turn right at the road. Continue ahead at the crossroads and go downhill into Wardlow.

5 Where the track ends, climb over a stile and follow the wall to your right for about 100 yards (90 m), then bear left downhill, crossing field boundaries by their stiles.

4 Turn left along a track at the picnic site and climb the rough wooded hillside.

3 Turn right along the walled lane as far as the picnic site.

10 Turn right at Upperdale Farm. Cross the river and climb up to the old railway line.

11 Go under a bridge, bear left, then turn right along the trail. Cross the viaduct and climb to the left, up the wooded slope to Monsal Head.

1 Walk down the Longstone road as far as the Packhorse Inn.

2 Turn left at the signpost to Chertpit Lane and Wardlow. Cross a series of small meadows using stiles in their boundaries.

Wardlow

PH

Hall Farm

Cressbrook Dale

370

Rolley Low

Ravensdale Cotts

Crossdale Head Mine (Opencast Workings)

Chertpit Plantation

Cressbrook Home Farm

Mill

Monsal Trail

Upperdale

Upperdale Farm

B 6465

River Wye

Monsal Head

PH

Little Longstone

PH

P

D

C

B

A

E

G

F

BLACK HARRY

5 miles (8 km) Easy/Moderate

Black Harry was an eighteenth-century highwayman who terrorized travellers on the rough roads and trackways around Longstone Edge and Coombs Dale above Stoney Middleton. He lived in a house which, even now, is a remote farmstead on Middleton Moor.

The walk starts in Eyam. Pronounced Eem, the name is thought to be Old English for an island, an apt description for a village which made a courageous stand against the plague between 1665 and 1666. Traditionally, it is thought that the virus came to Eyam, during late August 1665, in a box of cloth from London where the plague already had a tight hold. Starting in a cottage a few yards west of the church, the dread disease quickly spread throughout the village.

Led by their young rector, William Mompesson, and his non-conformist predecessor, Thomas Stanley, Eyam isolated itself from the outside world to contain the outbreak. They arranged for essential supplies of clothing, food, and medicine to be left at certain points around the village; payment was made by leaving money disinfected in vinegar. One such point was Mompesson's Well at the side of the road on to Eyam Edge, and another is thought to be the boundary stone which the walk passes on its way into Stoney Middleton.

Despite this act of herosim, 259 people died, including Mompesson's wife Katherine, and a total of seventy-six families were affected. Mompesson closed the church and held services in Cucklet Dell opposite the Hall. Burials were made in fields around family homes, and some of them can be seen on the walk. Every year on the last Sunday in August, a memorial service is held in Cucklet Dell.

Before starting the walk, spend a little time to explore this fascinating village. There is a fine example of a Saxon cross in the churchyard, and nearby is Katherine Mompesson's grave. Look also for the modern and amusing headstone on the grave of the Derbyshire cricketer, Harry Bagshaw.

Eyam is reached by a side road off the A623 which climbs leafy Eyam Dale. There is usually plenty of space in the car park next to the sports field along a side road to the west of the church.

A A group of headstones, known as Lydgate Graves, behind a low wall at the side of the lane tell the sad story of those who died from the plague in this corner of Eyam.

B To the left of the path an isolated gritstone boulder, the Boundary Stone, has a series of man-made holes in its upper surface, and is probably where money was left by the beleaguered villagers.

C Away from traffic on the A623, the village of Stoney Middleton is worth exploring. A well, still fed by a warm spring, is supposed to be on the site of a Roman bath. The rare octagonal church dates from 1759.

D Lead was once mined at Sallet Hole Mine but now fluorspar (calcium fluoride) – once a waste product – is extracted and used in the chemical and steel industries.

E The limestone uplands spread below this point. Black Harry was active on these narrow tracks; his house is hidden from view about $\frac{1}{4}$ mile (400 m) to the south-west. The grassy embankment at the side of the track is part of a slurry lagoon from the fluorspar-processing plant at Cavendish Mill across the moor.

F A partly grassed mound near the road junction was once a limekiln. An interpretive plaque explains its purpose.

G Darlton Quarry is to your right. From the track, you can see the massive limestone wall, a cross-section of the bed of a tropical sea which once covered this part of the Peak.

Over

0   1 mile
0   1 km

1 *Follow Lydgate until it turns sharp left at a group of farm cottages. Continue ahead along a field path.*

2 *Turn right on reaching the houses, then left and right again downhill along side lanes to the main road.*

3 *Cross the road and climb the tarmac path at the side of the Royal Oak. Turn right along the side road for a few yards, then left along a side lane.*

9 *Take care crossing the A623 and climb shaded Eyam Dale's road into the village.*

8 *Cross the road diagonally right and go down the rough track. Bear right, then left downhill past quarry buildings to the main road.*

4 *At the large house, turn right and follow the boundary wall. Go over a stile at the top of the field and bear left across a series of meadows.*

6 *Climb the stile on the right and bear right up the grassy hillside to a wall. Turn left and follow it uphill. (NB do not worry if you miss the stile, a right turn at the next track junction will lead to Point 7).*

5 *Go down the scrubby hillside, (slippery if wet) into narrow Coombs Dale. Turn right along the track.*

7 *Climb the stile and turn right along the rough track.*

P

Eyam

Town End

Lydgate Graves

B 6521

The Cliff

The Bank

A 623

Dale Brook

Stoney Middleton

Townend

Darlton Quarry

332

Coombs Dale

Black Harry Gate

Sallet Hole Mine

Ⓐ Ⓑ Ⓒ Ⓓ Ⓔ Ⓕ Ⓖ

35

FROGGATT EDGE

5½ miles (9 km) Moderate; one climb of 705 feet (215 m)

This is a walk full of contrasts and interest. Starting near the mouth of the longest and still-used railway tunnel in the Peak District, it passes some of the most natural woodland in the region and also the home of two Roman Catholic priests martyred for their beliefs. Valley strolling then follows and, after a short climb, an airy, rocky escarpment is reached where stonemasons once crafted millstones, the symbol of the Peak District National Park.

Access to the start of the walk is by the B6521 below the Fox House Inn on the Sheffield to Hope Valley road (A625). There is parking available on the side lane to Grindleford Station, which is served by Sheffield to Manchester trains. Alternatively, Sheffield to Bakewell buses stop at the lane end.

A An ancient oakwood fills Padley Gorge on the right. Its stream once powered a mill, now a private house on the far bank, at the side of the track.

B Padley Chapel is all that remains of an Elizabethan manor house. During the intolerant times of the late sixteenth-century, two devout Catholic families lived here. In 1588, two priests, Nicholas Garlick and Robert Ludlam, whom the family was sheltering, were captured and taken to Derby. There they were hanged, drawn, and quartered. The owner of the house, Thomas Fitzherbert, was taken to the Tower of London where he died in 1591. His brother, John, died in Fleet Prison seven years later. The house gradually fell into disrepair and eventually became farm buildings. Bought by the Nottingham Catholic Diocese in 1933, what was once a cowshed was converted into the chapel where pilgrimages are made every July. Brunt's Barn, a camping barn and National Park Ranger briefing centre, has been built nearby.

C The bay-windowed house beside the bridge on the B6521 over the River Derwent, was once a toll-house on the turnpike road between Bakewell and Sheffield which was built in the mid-eighteenth century.

D Well-worn stone flags and tiny clapper bridges indicate that the path through Froggatt Woods has been used for centuries.

E The coarse yet firm gritstone of the Derwent Edges was quarried for millstones, many of which litter the woodland and tumbled rocks below Froggatt Edge. The shape of the stones indicates their proposed use; some are bevelled and were for milling corn, others are broad and destined for sharpening Sheffield knives. The broadest were intended to be used as crushing rollers in the Scandinavian woodpulp industry, and these were still being supplied several years after World War 2. The Peak District National Park adopted the millstone as its logo, and several can be seen as you enter the National Park.

F The broad wooded Derwent Valley winds gently southwards on your left towards Chatsworth House and its splendid parkland. To the north and upstream, the high moors of the Dark Peak are marked by the prominent and shapely slopes of Win Hill, one of the true peaks in the Peak District. Further to the right are the main gritstone edges above the Derwent, with Higger Tor backing the enigmatic Iron Age fortress of Carl Wark.

G A path a few yards to the right leads through the heather to a small prehistoric stone circle topping a low earth bank, its purpose lost in the mists of time.

H Here is another glimpse of Higger Tor and the Eastern Edges through birch trees lining the rim of Froggatt Edge.

Over

36

0   1 mile

0   1 km

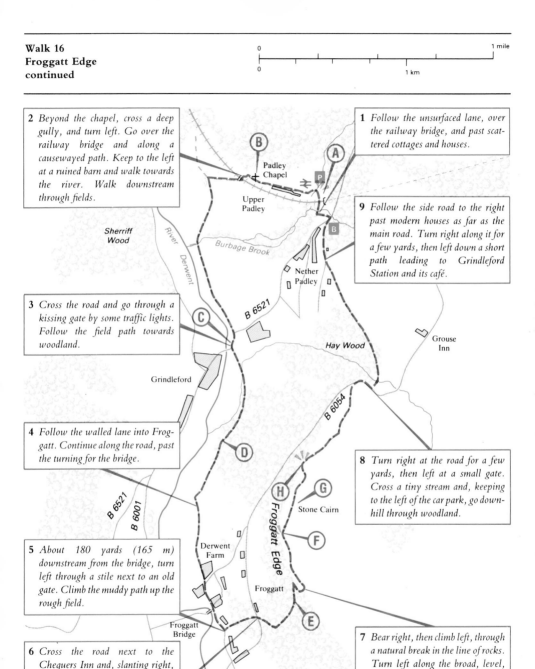

2 *Beyond the chapel, cross a deep gully, and turn left. Go over the railway bridge and along a causewayed path. Keep to the left at a ruined barn and walk towards the river. Walk downstream through fields.*

1 *Follow the unsurfaced lane, over the railway bridge, and past scattered cottages and houses.*

9 *Follow the side road to the right past modern houses as far as the main road. Turn right along it for a few yards, then left down a short path leading to Grindleford Station and its café.*

3 *Cross the road and go through a kissing gate by some traffic lights. Follow the field path towards woodland.*

4 *Follow the walled lane into Froggatt. Continue along the road, past the turning for the bridge.*

8 *Turn right at the road for a few yards, then left at a small gate. Cross a tiny stream and, keeping to the left of the car park, go downhill through woodland.*

5 *About 180 yards (165 m) downstream from the bridge, turn left through a stile next to an old gate. Climb the muddy path up the rough field.*

7 *Bear right, then climb left, through a natural break in the line of rocks. Turn left along the broad, level, crag-top path.*

6 *Cross the road next to the Chequers Inn and, slanting right, climb the woodland path.*

Padley Chapel

Upper Padley

Sherriff Wood

River Derwent

Burbage Brook

Nether Padley

B 6521

Grindleford

Hay Wood

Grouse Inn

B 6054

B 6521
B 6001

Stone Cairn

Froggatt Edge

Derwent Farm

Froggatt

Froggatt Bridge

37

Walk 17

ASHFORD LAKE

5½ miles (9 km) Easy

This walk, which can be extended by linking it with Walk 18, runs northwards from Bakewell to join the Monsal Trail and returns by way of Ashford-in-the-Water and its nearby lake. Several paths used on the walk were originally pack-horse ways, themselves based on some of the oldest tracks in the Peak. Monday is Bakewell's market day when parking can be a problem.

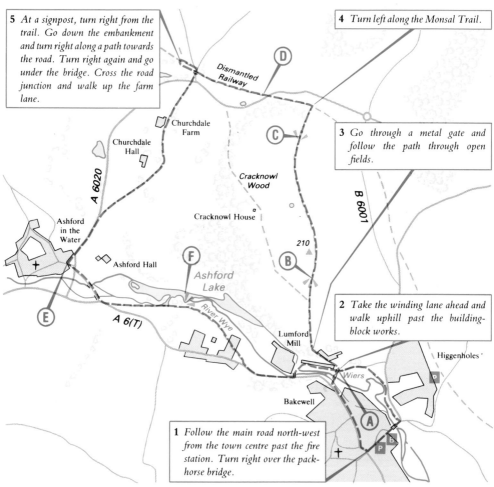

5 *At a signpost, turn right from the trail. Go down the embankment and turn right along a path towards the road. Turn right again and go under the bridge. Cross the road junction and walk up the farm lane.*

4 *Turn left along the Monsal Trail.*

3 *Go through a metal gate and follow the path through open fields.*

2 *Take the winding lane ahead and walk uphill past the building-block works.*

1 *Follow the main road north-west from the town centre past the fire station. Turn right over the pack-horse bridge.*

A Holme packhorse bridge was built in 1664.

B Look back on Bakewell sheltering in its sunny hollow.

C Look across Hassop Park to Longstone Edge. The roadside cottage below was a toll-house.

Over

0   1 mile

0   1 km

7 *Cross a stile, go downhill to the road, and turn left.*

6 *Follow the footpath sign to the left, then right around Churchdale Hall.*

8 *Turn right down a path at the first cottages in Ashford. Go to the left through the village. Cross the A6020 and go down the side road to cross the abandoned bridge.*

9 *Turn left along the main road for about 80 yards (73 m), then left through a kissing gate. Follow the path above the riverbank.*

10 *Go through a housing estate, across a narrow field to the road, and turn left.*

11 *At the mill, turn left over the bridge and then bear right through the car park. Follow the road past the turning to the pack-horse bridge and turn right at a kissing gate. Follow the path across the water meadows back to Bakewell.*

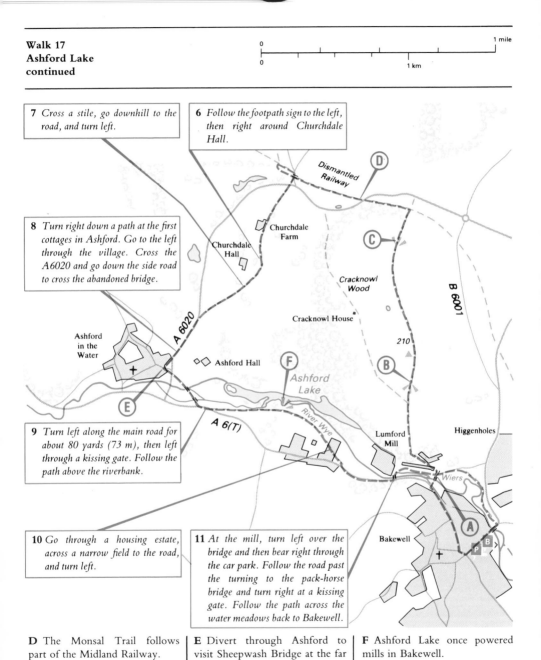

D The Monsal Trail follows part of the Midland Railway.

E Divert through Ashford to visit Sheepwash Bridge at the far end of the main street. There are several pubs and restaurants.

F Ashford Lake once powered mills in Bakewell.

Walk 18

THE DERBYSHIRE WYE AND HADDON HALL

$4\frac{1}{4}$ miles (7 km) Easy

Intended either as a separate walk or linked with Walk 17, the route is through watermeadows beside the Wye downstream from Bakewell to the unchanged medieval baronial hall of Haddon. On the return leg, woodland and field paths are followed to the west of the river and also the A6.

The walk starts in Bakewell from the seventeenth-century Market House, now a Peak District National Park Information Centre near the market place.

Buses from Matlock, Buxton, Sheffield, and the surrounding villages serve Bakewell. There is a large car park in the market place and also space on the opposite side of the river. Roads around the town can be rather congested on market days which are held every Monday.

A The town of Bakewell grew around a crossing place on the River Wye defended by a castle built in 942. The first recorded name was the Saxon *Badecean Wiellon*, 'Beadeca's spring'. The spring never became popular, mainly because it was colder than that at nearby Buxton. Bath Gardens, always immaculate in the town centre, and the seventeenth-century Bath house are the remains of a failed scheme to make Bakewell into a spa.

The castle was a simple wooden stockade on top of a mound to the east of the river, and Bakewell was important enough to be recorded in the *Domesday* survey. The market received its charter in 1330 and has been on its present riverside site, supplying the needs of visitors and locals, since 1826. Sheep and cattle are brought in from all around the district and, together with traders' stalls, they help to build up an atmosphere every Monday which is one of chaotic, but friendly activity.

Surrounded by interesting old buildings, the parish church has looked down on Bakewell since Saxon times. Inside, many ancient stones and relics tell its history. Dorothy Vernon and her husband John Manners are buried in the Vernon chapel. Uphill, a little way from the church, and along an alley is the Old House Museum, an interesting collection of local artifacts.

A little way north along the A6 from the town centre, and close by mills established by Richard Arkwright in the eighteenth century, is a narrow four-arched, pack-horse bridge, built in 1664 and only just wide enough to take a pony with its panniers.

Spend a little time wandering along the river bank watching for trout, or feeding the ducks.

B Look across the watermeadows to the Derbyshire Wye. The well-stocked river is the popular venue of trout fishermen.

C An attractive view of Haddon Hall can be glimpsed through trees from this point. This perfect example of a medieval manor house owes its preservation to the fact that its owners, the Manners (Earls, then Dukes, of Rutland) moved from here to Belvoir Castle, Leicestershire in the seventeenth century. Earlier this century, the father of the present Duke began the process of restoration to make Haddon unique among the stately homes of Britain. Entering through a cobbled courtyard, the visitor moves into a bygone age when Sir John Manners was able to hold extended Christmas parties in the magnificent banqueting hall, or perhaps walk the long gallery where Dorothy Vernon planned to elope with her lover, an earlier John Manners. Formal rose gardens at the side of the house make an excellent vantage point for views of the wooded river.

D From here, you can look back on one of the most attractive views of Haddon Hall.

E The Wye Valley is below, with Longstone Edge making the skyline. Bakewell fits well into this scene, with the tip of the church spire marking its position on a hillside to the left of the town centre.

Over

40

Bakewell

(A) **P**

(B)

1 *Walk through the market place to the river and turn right, then left across two footbridges. Follow a wide track to the right.*

2 *Go through a gate and follow a waymarked grassy path.*

3 *Cross a narrow footbridge and, ignoring the arrow pointing left, walk downstream.*

4 *Do not cross the anglers' stile, but follow the fence as indicated by waymarks.*

12 *Cross the road diagonally left and go through a stile. Follow the path through allotment gardens and past houses to the park. Cross the park and turn left at the river, following it upstream to Bakewell Market.*

11 *Follow a hedge, then turn right downhill along a farm lane to the road.*

River Wye

A 6(T)

Haddon House

Burton Ashes Wood

Wiggen Dale

Dismantled Railway

5 *Go through the gate and turn right, along a lane for a few yards, then left over a metal stile. Walk through woodland by the side of the river.*

10 *Follow the wood's lower boundary. Cross a footbridge, and walk towards another wood at the top of the rise. Enter and leave the wood by stiles.*

(E)

(C)

Haddon Park

Haddon Hall

9 *Keep to the right of the plantation and cross the stile near a field corner. Go to the right, downhill into the wooded side dale.*

Haddon Barn

Haddon Fields

(D)

8 *At a fingerpost near the small circular wood, turn right across pathless fields, using stiles to cross boundaries.*

7 *Cross the road and follow the right-hand of two pointers, uphill on a wide field track.*

6 *Cross the river, climb up to the main road, and turn left.*

Walk 19

CALTON LEES AND EDENSOR

6 miles (9½ km) Easy

The walk is around a series of plantations and home farms belonging to Chatsworth Park, seat of the Dukes of Devonshire. On the return, the route is through Edensor, the purpose-built estate village, and then the River Derwent is followed downstream through unspoilt parkland. There is a large free car park at the Beeley end of Chatsworth Park.

Allow plenty of time on this walk to include a visit to Chatsworth House and its gardens. The house is usually open between March and October, but check locally.

8 *Turn right at the fork and go down the tree-lined, unmetalled lane.*

9 *Walk through the village and cross the road. Follow a gravel-surfaced path to the right across the hillside.*

10 *Turn right and follow the river downstream.*

7 *Go down a walled track and turn right along the road for about ¼ mile (800 m).*

11 *Go past the first weir and turn right. Climb steadily uphill to the road and turn left. Go through a gate next to the cattle grid. The car park is on the right.*

1 *Follow the lane away from the car park and to the right of the garden centre. Bear right past the estate saw-mill into the tree-lined valley.*

6 *Go between a pond and an isolated clump of trees to follow a gradually developing path.*

2 *Continue ahead at the fork along an unsurfaced track.*

5 *Aim uphill for a prominent mound and turn right. There is no clear path but, keeping the tops of trees just in sight on your left, look ahead for stiles in two field boundaries.*

4 *Turn sharp left in the gap between two plantations. Cross a stile and follow the left-hand wall for about 150 yards (137 m). Turn right, uphill.*

3 *Zig-zag uphill to the left of estate cottages and, where the track turns right, go through a gate on the left to follow a grassy path beside a fir plantation.*

Map labels: B 6048, Chatsworth House, Edensor, River Derwent, 280, Moatless Plantation, New Piece Wood, B 6012, Bakewell, River Wye, Calton Houses, Calton Pastures, Calton Lees, Lees Wood, Calton Lees Farm, Beeley Lodge, D, C, A, E, B, P

A Look across the Derwent to the steep valley holding Hell Bank Plantation. Heather-covered Beeley Moor is beyond.

B Look eastwards across New Piece Wood to the Derwent and its craggy escarpments.

C Bakewell is below, and beyond it the rolling uplands of the White Peak.

D To the right of the road junction, look over the wall on the left where an old road marker indicates the once greater importance of the lane as part of the Bakewell to Chatsworth turnpike.

E Edensor village (pron. 'Ensor') originally stood between the river and the B6012, but was moved to its present position between 1838 and 1842 so as not to impede the view from Chatsworth House.

Walk 20

ROYSTONE GRANGE

4½ miles (7¼ km) Easy

0					1 mile
0			1 km		

This walk visits a farming settlement whose occupation can be traced from prehistoric and Roman times to the present day.

A booklet describing these features is available from the Peak District National Park. The walk begins from Minninglow car park

½ mile (800 m) south of the A5012.

2 *Climb to the left at a fingerpost. Cross the stile and walk across a series of fields.*

1 *Turn left along the High Peak Trail and follow the track bed through woodland.*

8 *Go through a gate and turn right along the trail. Follow it back to the car park.*

Gotham

(A)

P

High Peak Trail

Minninglow Grange

Roystone Cottages

372

7 *Climb the stile and turn left along the grassy lane.*

6 *Cross a stone stile on the left and turn right uphill along a footpath towards, and under, the old railway line.*

3 *Climb over the stile and, following waymarks, turn left along the lane. Cross the road to go down the lane opposite.*

(F)

(B) Quarries (disused)

Minninglow Hill

Roystone Rocks

Roystone Grange (E)

(C)

5 *After visiting the medieval grange and Roman fields, walk back towards the farm. Do not re-enter the yard, but turn right and cross a stile. Follow the field path across the grassy depression.*

4 *Turn right at the junction and follow the farm lane to Roystone Grange.*

(D)

A The High Peak Trail continues around Gotham Curve. Once part of the Cromford and High Peak Railway, linking canals at Cromford and Whaley Bridge, the bend was one of the sharpest on any standard-gauge line, and rolling stock had short wheel bases.

B Traces of a Roman farm can be seen on the right of the track as you approach the eighteenth-century Roystone Grange.

C Beyond the farmyard is a chapel-like structure, once a compressor house. Near it are the remains of a medieval grange.

D Lower down the track are the terraces of Roman fields.

E As you walk towards Point 6, study the walls, parts of which date from the twelfth-century.

F On the left are the remains of a Victorian brickworks.

Walk 21

STANTON MOOR

4¼ miles (7 km) Easy

This isolated gritstone moorland plateau, an inlier within the limestone White Peak, is only about a mile (1½ km) long by a little over ½ mile (800 m) at its widest, but it held tremendous significance to the people who lived nearby during the Bronze Age. They built no fewer than five circles — some are of stones and some earth banks – and at least seventy burial mounds can be found scattered around the heather moor. A number of enigmatic standing stones point towards distant prominences. Many of the mounds, or tumuli, have been disturbed. Stones, which once formed a neat, grassed-over cairn, lie scattered around their tops. This is mostly the result of sometimes inexpert excavations carried out by locals from the nearby village of Birchover in the earlier part of this century.

Birchover is traditionally the home of quarrymen, many of whom still work the warm-hued building stone of the quarry that stands between the moor and the village. The walk starts and finishes in Birchover where there are two hospitable inns.

Moving into prehistoric times across Stanton Moor, the walk returns to the twentieth century along a pack-horse way which, for generations, saw loads of Cheshire salt en route for Derbyshire and South Yorkshire.

Approach Birchover by a side road south-east off the B5056, Bakewell to Ashbourne road. There is usually ample parking space along the main street in the village. A weekday bus service between Bakewell and Matlock passes through Birchover.

A The Cork Stone. Iron rungs set into the face of this rock enable adventurous spirits to climb to its narrow summit. A circular basin on top of the rock hints of some ancient sacrificial rite.

B Nine Ladies stone circle. This lonely little group and its attendant King Stone are supposed to be a group of ladies and a fiddler who were turned to stone because they danced on the Sabbath. Probably of religious significance, the most plausible explanation for the stone circle is that it was some form of astronomical calendar. A little to the west is an oval-shaped earth bank and, further on, another is in the form of a complete circle.

C The moor-edge Earl Grey's Tower was erected in 1832 to commemorate Earl Grey's involvement in the passing of the Reform Act.

D The Derwent Valley is below. To your left, the position of Chatsworth House can usually be noted from the spray of the Emperor Fountain, the second highest in Europe. Beyond Chatsworth are the outcrops and edges lining the valley rim. To your right is Matlock, dominated by the ruin of Riber Castle.

E The skyline on the right is dotted by ancient tumuli. Relics found during excavations in the 1920s can be seen in the Sheffield City Museum.

F South-facing Birchover is on the right, sheltering beneath the wooded slopes of Barton Hill. Winster and Elton, two former lead-mining villages, are on your left. The lane you have recently joined and also the cart track and footpath beyond Point 7, were once part of a pack-horse way from Cheshire to South Yorkshire. The route can still be traced as a footpath, east to Darley Bridge and west by way of Robin Hood's Stride to Middleton-by-Youlgreave.

G Rowtor Rocks are on the left. A place of fanciful, druidical legend, many of the stones were carved into caves and seats in the eighteenth century by an eccentric local vicar, the Reverend Thomas Eyre. The tiny chapel is well worth a visit. Inside it has some excellent wood carvings and primitive wall paintings, together with a memorial to Joan Waste who, aged 22, was burned at the stake in the Windmill Pit, Derby in 1555 for her protestant beliefs.

Over

0   1 mile

0   1 km

2 *Turn right beneath a beech tree and go past a large boulder. Climb over the stile and follow a sandy path upwards to the moor. Turn left at the aptly named Cork Stone, then right to follow a moorland path past the triangulation point.*

3 *Bear left through a birch grove and right at a path crossing. Go over a stile and bear right along the moorland edge.*

4 *Follow the boundary fence to the right.*

1 *Cross the road opposite the Druid Inn and climb the woodland path above Birchover. Turn left opposite the quarry entrance and walk along the road for 300 yards (275 m).*

Nine Ladies
Stone Circle

King's
Stone

Ⓑ Ⓒ Ⓓ

**Stanton
Moor**

Ⓐ

▲ 323

Ⓔ

Cork Stone

Stanton Park
Quarry

Barn Farm

B 5056

Ⓖ

Birchover

Rocking Stone
Farm

Upper Town

Uppertown
Farm

Ⓕ

5 *Go down to the road and turn right for about 200 yards (180 m). Turn left at a stile beneath an oak tree and go down to the farm. Keep to the left of the main buildings and continue ahead at a three-way signpost, across two fields, keeping close to the hedge.*

8 *Turn right at the stile in front of a large house. Go down the drive and turn right, uphill along an unsurfaced lane into Birchover.*

7 *Turn left along the road for a few yards and pass a group of houses. Cross a stile on the right and follow a cart track for a little way, then go ahead by a field path.*

6 *Go through a stile and turn right along a farm lane.*

Walk 22
WINSTER
5½ (9 km) Easy/Moderate

Winster is a haphazard cluster of seventeenth- and eighteenth-century houses linked by narrow hillside alleys or ginnels, a system which suited the lead miners and their families in the hey-day of this now extinguished Peak District industry. The walk follows paths once trodden by miners who, usually in small groups, mined beneath the surrounding heights. Often run on a part-time basis, the miners would be satisfied with enough ore to fill their wes'kit (waistcoat) pockets after a day underground. Small abandoned stone barns, or coes, used as stores by these miners, still dot the fields. At the side of the B5056, close to its junction with the Newhaven road, a communal lead store has been preserved as an interpretive feature. A little way down the road, the Miners' Standard Inn takes its name from a standard dish which was used to measure quantities of ore.

In contrast with this small-time mining activity, the last and most productive mine in Derbyshire was nearby at Mill Close. It was still in operation until 1939 when disastrous floods led to its abandon.

The main feature in Winster is its two-storey, late seventeenth-century Market Hall. The once open ground floor was bricked up to strengthen the structure when the upper floor was added. This is also in brick, an unusual feature in an area of plentiful building stone. The Market Hall was the first property in Derbyshire to be owned by the National Trust. There is a small information centre on the upper floor. Winster has its own team of Morris Dancers, and every Shrovetide the women and children hold pancake races.

Parking is difficult in the centre of Winster, but can usually be found to the west (Elton) side of the church, or above the village near the Miners' Standard. The Matlock to Elton bus runs through Winster.

A From fields disturbed by ancient mining activity, look across the wooded valley to Stanton Moor. To your left are Cratcliffe Rocks and Robin Hood's Stride, the latter once known as Mock Beggar's Hall from its apparent shape as a mansion when viewed in poor light at dusk. Beyond these two groups of rocks, the trough of Lathkill Dale cuts into the high limestone plateau of the White Peak. On the right of the view is Clough Wood where once busy Mill Close Mine's remains blend into the now mature woodland. Look right again to where the deep, wide Derwent Valley carves its way past Chatsworth and on into the gritstone highlands of the Dark Peak.

B A fenced-off area below the wooded outcrop of Luntor Rocks marks the site of an old mine shaft. Most, but not all, shafts are blanked off with concrete beams or by beehive cairns. **Treat every mineshaft with respect for many have unstable sides.**

C The factory is a hi-tech metal recovery plant on the site of the new Mill Close Mine, the last productive lead mine in the Peak District. At the height of its productive capacity, the mine was one of the biggest in the world and produced almost half-a-million tons of ore during its lifetime. Always beset by flooding, the first Mill Close shaft was sunk in woodland a little to the south-west of Point 9, and, in fact, is passed on the way to Point 10. Starting in the 1700s, Mill Close had a chequered career until the mid-nineteenth century when more efficient pumping equipment made mining its ores viable again. The new mine was created by sinking a shaft near Warren Carr on the far side of the factory in 1874, followed by a second in 1881. Despite all efforts, a particularly bad series of floods in 1938 and 1939 led to the mine finally being abandoned.

Surface remains of the Old Mill Close Mine have been preserved by the Peak District Historical Mines Association.

Over

9 *Climb a stile and turn left uphill along the lane. Fork left at the lane end, to bear left along a woodland track. Do not cross the stream, but keep to its right along the valley.*

8 *Cross two fields and turn left along the forest track.*

7 *Follow the narrow street to the main road. Cross and, keeping to the right of the cottage opposite, follow the signposted path to Stanton Moor and Birchover.*

10 *Follow a path along the wooded valley bottom. Cross the stream and go over a stile. Using two old gate posts and stone stiles to indicate the way, go half-right then diagonally left uphill.*

Clough Wood

Cambridge Wood

11 *Cross the stile and turn right along the road into Winster.*

225

Wensley

Painters Way Farm

B 5057

Big Dungeon

Wensley Dale

Little Dungeon

Winster

A

B

Luntor Rocks

6 *Turn left along a walled track. Cross the dry dale and climb to the right towards the village.*

1 *Walk up the side street from the Market Place. Turn left at Hope Cottage and follow a path signposted to Bonsall. Bear left along the narrow alley, then, using stiles, climb diagonally right across a series of fields.*

Tearsall Farm

5 *Bear right, downhill at the path junction, as indicated by a yellow arrow, and head for a ruined barn.*

Brightgate Farm

2 *Go through a stile in the wall on your right and turn left, to follow the wall across the bottom of three fields. Then, following waymarks, incline right.*

3 *Go diagonally across the level field to a stile in its far corner. Cross and turn left along the road.*

4 *By the weight-restriction sign, turn left down the first of two adjacent tracks. Keep to the right of the farm and, following blue waymarks, bear left and walk round the lip of the quarry.*

MIDDLETON AND LONG DALE

6 miles (9½ km) Easy

Two little-known White Peak dales are explored on this walk from the secluded village of Middleton-by-Youlgreave. The first, Bradford Dale, has a river but Long Dale is dry. Between them, high limestone pastures are crossed along the way, offering wide-ranging views over the surrounding countryside.

Middleton might seem a sleepy place today, but it has seen plenty of activity down the centuries. It once had a castle although nothing remains apart from a mound and, during the English Civil War, a bloody skirmish took place nearby. Thomas Bateman, the nineteenth-century archaeologist who explored many of the ancient stones and tumuli on the surrounding moors of the Peak District (some say with an over-heavy hand more in search of treasure than information), came from Lomberdale Hall and is buried in the village. His tomb can be found at the end of a track signposted from the old Wesleyan chapel. A stone replica of a Neolithic burial urn adorns the lid of the tomb.

A A partly overgrown pond in the dale bottom is the upper of a series of small reservoirs. Now the home of trout, the river was dammed creating water power to drive a lead-crushing mill at Alport lower down the dale.

B The underlying strata on your side of the stream dip sharply towards Rowlow Brook. Rocks on the far side of the brook have been worn into overhangs by water action, partly by the stream, but mostly by floodwater at the end of the Ice Age.

C Look back along the way you have come. Bradford Dale points towards the prominent square tower of Youlgreave Church. Beyond and across the deep trough of the Derwent Valley, wooded slopes above Chatsworth climb towards heather-clad Beeley Moor, a purple riot every summer.

D Almost secretive Long Dale is below, a completely dry dale supporting short but succulent grazing. On the opposite hillside are humps and hollows, the remains of trial holes from a time when the White Peak yielded its hoard of lead ore. Over to the left and on the highest point of the skyline, a lonely clump of trees marks the site of Minninglow, the largest and most important tumulus in the Peak. In May and June look for the tiny, pansy-like flower known locally as 'Heart's ease'; *Viola tricolor* is usually blue but it is sometimes yellow in the limestone dales of the Peak District.

E Bradford Dale reappears below and leads the eye towards the Derwent's heather moors. Land on your left and right is based on limestone all the way to Elton, the former mining village on the far right. The opposite, or southern, side of Bradford Dale is mostly grit-stone as indicated by a proliferation of trees which grow best on the moister and acidic soils based on a foundation of grit-stone.

Over

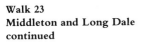

0   1 mile

0   1 km

1 Go down the lane opposite the playground into Bradford Dale, and turn right.

2 Cross the footbridge and climb the slope, then down again to recross the stream, by a stone-slab bridge. Cross the next fields by using stiles in their walls.

3 Go over the narrow lane to follow a tiny brook upstream. Where it bends to your left, continue ahead, to the right, above a wooded ravine.

10 Turn right at the road and walk downhill into Middleton.

9 Turn right along the farm lane. Where it forks, beyond a large sycamore, bear left along a walled lane.

4 Turn left along the road.

5 Where the road bends sharply left, continue ahead and uphill, along the sunken track.

6 Drop steeply into Long Dale. Turn right along the dale bottom. Bear left at the first clump of trees. Cross a stile and go to the right along a narrow field between two sets of woodland. Go through an old gateway and follow the grassy track parallel to the field.

8 Go over a stone stile on the right and cross five fields, using stiles to find the route.

7 Climb up to the road and turn right along it for a little under ½ mile (800 m).

Castle (rems of)

Batemans Tomb

Middleton

Rake Wood

Middleton Hall

(A)

(E)

(B)

Woodside Farm

Kenslow Wood

Kenslow Farm

Kingham Low

Smerrill Grange

△ 325

Bolderstone Plantation

Little Bolderstone Plantation

Long Dale

(C)

(D)

Walk 24

RIBER AND DETHICK

5 miles (8 km) Easy

Only the façade of Riber Castle is left standing. Built by John Smedley in the 1850s as a hydropathic establishment, it never succeeded, mainly because it lacked a good water supply! From the castle, the route uses quiet paths to reach Dethick, and starts high above Matlock but, as an alternative, the walk may be extended from the centre of Matlock by way of Starkholmes and climbing the steep path from the road to the castle.

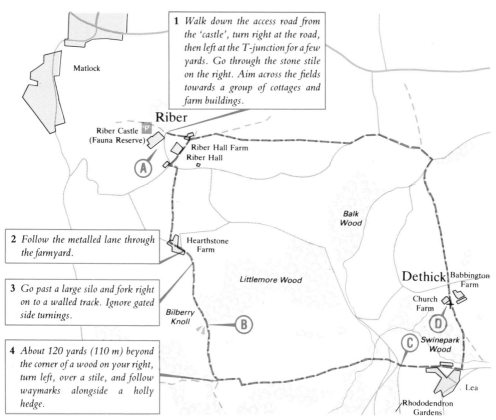

1 *Walk down the access road from the 'castle', turn right at the road, then left at the T-junction for a few yards. Go through the stone stile on the right. Aim across the fields towards a group of cottages and farm buildings.*

2 *Follow the metalled lane through the farmyard.*

3 *Go past a large silo and fork right on to a walled track. Ignore gated side turnings.*

4 *About 120 yards (110 m) beyond the corner of a wood on your right, turn left, over a stile, and follow waymarks alongside a holly hedge.*

A Most of the older buildings in Riber are Elizabethan or Jacobean, and the Hall is now a high-class hotel. After years of neglect, the castle now houses an interesting zoo specializing mainly in endangered species and European wildlife. Following a successful breeding programme, the zoo has exported lynx to national parks in France and Spain where they are released into the wild.

B The little hill you have just climbed is Bilberry Knoll; clumps of this succulent fruit grow at the side of the track. Ahead, the wooded Derwent winds its way southwards, and to the left is Crich Stand with its

Over

50

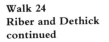

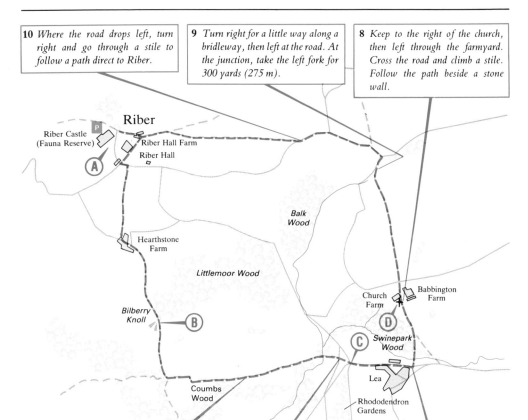

10 *Where the road drops left, turn right and go through a stile to follow a path direct to Riber.*

9 *Turn right for a little way along a bridleway, then left at the road. At the junction, take the left fork for 300 yards (275 m).*

8 *Keep to the right of the church, then left through the farmyard. Cross the road and climb a stile. Follow the path beside a stone wall.*

Riber

Riber Castle (Fauna Reserve)
Riber Hall Farm
Riber Hall
A

Balk Wood

Hearthstone Farm

Littlemoor Wood

Church Farm
Babbington Farm
D

Bilberry Knoll
B

C
Swinepark Wood

Coumbs Wood

Lea

Rhododendron Gardens

5 *Follow the waymarks to the left, across two fields. Turn right into woodland and go down to stepping stones across a stream. Climb up to the road.*

6 *Follow the path between two roads. Go through a stile and ahead into Lea village.*

7 *Turn left at a kissing gate and follow a footpath, signposted to Dethick and Tansley, across the deep, wooded dell. Continue by field path.*

lighthouse memorial to the men of the Sherwood Foresters who died in both world wars. Crich Tramway Museum is in the quarry below the lighthouse.

C A diversion of about

350 yards (320 m) to the right leads to Lea Rhododendron Gardens which are highly recommended in early summer.

D The sleepy hamlet of Dethick was the home of the Babbing-

tons who tried to free Mary Queen of Scots during her imprisonment at nearby Wingfield Manor. All that is left of what was once a small settlement are three farms and a church.

Walk 25

BIGGIN DALE AND IRON TORS

6½ miles (10½ km) Easy

The walk is from Biggin, a village which appears to spread itself in leisurely fashion across the limestone plateau a couple of miles south-east of Hartington. Below is its dale, a tributary of the Dove; both are followed as far as the wooded outcrop of Iron Tors, and the return is along part of the Tissington Trail.

Biggin has regular sheep sales, one attractive pub, and a café or two to provide refreshment at the end of the walk. Parking is along the roadside away from field gates or private driveways.

3 *Turn left along the road for about 100 yards (90 m). Turn right at a stile, heading downhill along a grassy path.*

2 *Go through a stile on the left and cross two fields, passing farm buildings, and aiming for a gap among a group of cottages.*

1 *Walk south along the side road past Biggin Church, following it to the right at the far end.*

4 *Turn left along the dale bottom.*

10 *At a complex of wall junctions, bear half-right across the next field, then follow a walled lane as far as the road. Turn right for the church.*

5 *Turn left and follow the wooded riverbank downstream.*

9 *Where the trail crosses an unsurfaced track, turn left and go down to, then over, the track. Follow yellow waymarks, stiles, and gates across a series of fields.*

6 *Do not cross the footbridge on your right, but carry on downstream for a few more yards, then turn left to climb the craggy side dale.*

7 *Leave the dale head and turn right along the road.*

8 *At the bridge, turn right and climb the embankment, then left along the trail.*

Map labels: Biggin · Dalehead · River Dove · Biggin Dale · Cave · A · B · C · D · E · 370 · Tissington Trail · Dismtd Rly · Lees Barn · A 515 · Iron Tors · Coldeaton Bridge

A Stray animals were once kept in the round walled enclosure which has been rebuilt adjacent to the village hall. Their owners had to pay a fine to the Pinder to secure their release.

B Biggin Dale is a nature reserve where many attractive plants bloom on the sparse limestone soil of the hillsides, or in damp shady places.

C The cave-like hole on the left was a trial hole for a lead mine that never developed. Although it looks artificial, the dale-side scree is natural.

D Dove Dale describes a series of interconnecting dales, all with a separate character. Izaak Walton and his friend, Charles Cotton, fished for the trout in these still-clear waters.

E The Tissington Trail follows part of an old railway which once linked Ashbourne and Buxton.

Walk 26
ILAM AND THE LOWER
MANIFOLD VALLEY
4¼ miles (7 km) Easy

0					1 mile
0			1 km		

On this walk the River Manifold is followed for a little way above Ilam Country Park, and the return is across farmland. Relics of St Bertram, who brought Christianity to this corner of the Peak, are visited along the way.

There is a car park in front of the hall as well as an information centre, shop, and tea rooms. Part of the riverside path upstream of the hall is private, but public access is allowed on payment of a small toll.

5 Turn right along the road to the second of two farm drives on the left.

Moor Barn

Castern Hall

D

6 Turn left across a cattle grid. Follow the lane for a few yards, then bear right towards the left-hand edge of woodland.

7 Go over a stile and begin to descend to the right, below the hillside. Turn sharp right at the second stile and go steeply into the dry valley.

E

River Lodge

4 Go to the right of the hall. Turn right at a gate and follow the direction of the signpost to Ilam Moor.

C

River Dove

F

▲ 329

Bunster Hill
St Bertrams Well

3 Turn left at the cottage. Follow the road and turn right at the fork.

Ilam Estate Country Park

8 Go down to the road and turn right. Bear right again through the village, and left towards the church and Ilam Hall.

2 Go through an iron squeezer stile and continue to follow the river-bank.

B **P** **A** **i**
Ilam Hall
Cross   St Bertrams Bridge

1 Walk down to the river and turn right along a wide level path.

A The Victorian Ilam Hall, now a Youth Hostel, as well as the village are owned by the National Trust. The Hall and village were built on the site of an earlier manor.

B Hinkley Wood is opposite, and a tenth-century Saxon Battle Cross stands at the side of Paradise Walk.

C The river is wide and deep near Ilam, but here it flows mostly underground from Wetton, 4 miles (6½ km) upstream.

D Most of the nearby farms are built on ancient foundations. Throwley Hall, opposite, has a fortified tower.

E Ilam Country park is below with Bunster Hill left.

F St Bertram is supposed to have baptized people at this hillside well.

Walk 27
THE HAMPS AND MANIFOLD VALLEYS
4½ miles (7¼ km) Easy

Until 1934, a narrow-gauge railway ran along the Upper Manifold and Hamps valleys. From its terminus at Hulme End, it ran to Waterhouses where the specially constructed rolling stock was loaded on to standard-gauge waggons. This walk follows part of the track and returns by a high-level bridleway.

Park at Weag's Bridge on the Wetton to Grindon road.

9 Follow the road downhill, around the hairpin, and turn right at a stile next to a ruined barn. Bear left downhill into the valley. The exit stile is partly hidden by hawthorns close to the bridge.

1 Go through the gate marked by a vehicle restriction sign and follow the narrow tarmacked track.

8 Turn left at a gate uphill to the road, and turn right.

7 Turn right at a big old tree and aim to the left of a stone barn. Then go into the dry, shallow valley.

2 Follow the track to the right into the wooded side valley.

6 Follow an old hawthorn hedge, then walls to the right across fields. Again, use narrow gates to keep to the route.

5 Go past the remote farmhouse to cross a shallow valley by a grassy track. Zig-zag up the far side.

3 Turn right opposite a footbridge to Lee House Tea Room, and go through a kissing gate. Turn sharp right uphill. Go through two gates and into woodland. Beyond the wood, the path is indistinct, but narrow gates point the way.

4 Turn right along a farm lane.

Weag's Bridge · P · A · Beeston Tor · Manifold · B · Beeston Tor Farm · D · C · Old Soles Wood · River Hamp · 335 · Hell Hole · Throwley Moor · Little Wood · Lee House

A The Manifold Valley is usually dry in summer, flowing underground from Wetton Mill to Ilam.

B Look eastwards across the Manifold Valley to the dramatic crag of Beeston Tor.

C Apart from the railway, the narrow Hamps Valley has not been changed by humans and, as a result, wildlife is abundant.

D This offers a higher-level view across the Manifold and Beeston Tor. Hummocky hills on the skyline were once coral reefs in a tropical sea when Britain was part of a continent to the south of the equator.

Walk 28

BRAND TOP

3 miles (5 km) Moderate

Small hill farms and remote cottages feature on this walk around a little-known part of the Peak District. Ancient footpaths criss-cross the area around the headwaters of the Dove, paths and trackways which were once the commercial arteries of the Peak and echoed to the sound of pack-ponies. The walk starts at Brandside. Follow the signposted road south from the A53, Buxton to Leek road, across Axe Edge, and park near the war memorial at the road end.

1 Go down the road from the war memorial, through a gate, and ahead along a farm track.

2 Follow the track to the right downhill, then left almost to the stream.

3 Bear left downstream. The path is indistinct at first, but one develops along a grassy terrace. Stiles mark the way.

4 Go steeply into the side valley. Climb a stile and cross a stone footbridge by the main stream. Walk downstream, and then right along a cobbled bridleway.

5 Do not cross the narrow bridge but turn left and cross a stile. Go past a barn and bear left uphill over three rough fields. Join a wall and follow it to a farm.

6 Follow the access lane away from the farm.

7 Keep to the right at the next farm as far as a duck pond. Turn left, cross a stile, and walk back towards the farm. Follow a fence away and use further stiles in field boundaries.

8 Continue ahead and slightly uphill at the fingerpost along an improving path.

9 Turn left away from the track. There is no path, but follow a wall and cross a plank bridge. Bear right up the shallow valley.

10 Turn left over a footbridge. Ignoring the stile in front, turn sharp right and follow a wire fence uphill. Bear right along a farm lane, then right again to reach Brand Top.

Brand Top

A

Howe Green

Brand End

D

400

Booth Farm

Leycote

B

C

Tenterhill

A Rocky hills on the opposite side of the valley of Upper Dovedale were once coral reefs. This side of the valley is shale from an ancient river bed; the other is limestone.

B Born amid the shales of Axe Edge, the River Dove reaches the limestone dale below Hollinsclough a little over a mile (1½ km) to the south.

C Countless trains of pack-ponies, carrying Cheshire salt to Derbyshire and South Yorkshire have worn the cobbles of this graceful, single-arched bridge.

D Notice the change of stone used in the walls. The division between brown gritstone and the white limestone is abrupt.

Walk 29

FERNILEE

5 miles (8 km) Moderate; one climb of 394 feet (120 m)

A woodland stroll beside an attractive reservoir, followed by an easy climb, lead to delightful views of the Goyt Valley.

Access is down the steep side road from the top of Long Hill (A5002) Buxton to Whaley Bridge road. Park at the Errwood car park and picnic site on the opposite side of the dam. The access road follows part of the Bunsal Incline on the old High Peak Railway. Waggons were lowered and raised by a system of stationary engines.

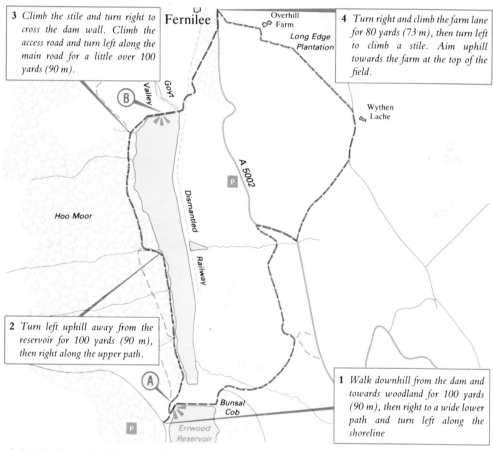

3 *Climb the stile and turn right to cross the dam wall. Climb the access road and turn left along the main road for a little over 100 yards (90 m).*

4 *Turn right and climb the farm lane for 80 yards (73 m), then turn left to climb a stile. Aim uphill towards the farm at the top of the field.*

2 *Turn left uphill away from the reservoir for 100 yards (90 m), then right along the upper path.*

1 *Walk downhill from the dam and towards woodland for 100 yards (90 m), then right to a wide lower path and turn left along the shoreline*

Fernilee

Overhill Farm

Long Edge Plantation

Wythen Lache

Goyt Valley

Hoo Moor

Dismantled Railway

A 5002

Bunsal Cob

Errwood Reservoir

A It is hard to realize that a self-supporting estate with its own coal mines once occupied the upper part of the Goyt Valley. All that remains are the ruins of Errwood Hall and the family graves of the Grimshaws in a side valley to the west of Errwood Reservoir. The road climbing to the west, and away from the reservoir, is thought to be based on a Roman road linking Chester (*Deva*) and Buxton (*Aquae Arnemetiae*). An interpretive plaque near the car park

Over

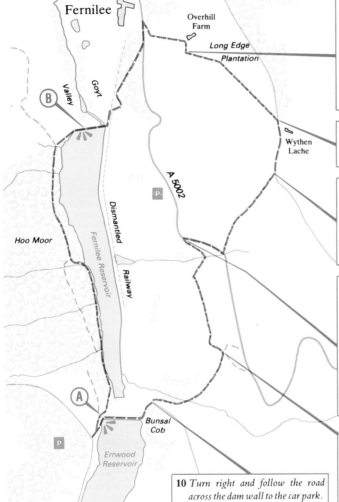

Fernilee

Overhill Farm

Long Edge Plantation

Goyt Valley

B

Wythen Lache

A 5002

Dismantled Railway

Fernilee Reservoir

Hoo Moor

A

Bunsal Cob

Errwood Reservoir

5 *At the farm, go over the stile and turn right, along the lane for few yards, then left uphill on a field track as indicated by yellow waymarks. Bear right beyond the top of the first field and aim for the right-hand edge of the skyline wood.*

6 *Go over the stile and turn right along the narrow road for about ¼ mile (400 m).*

7 *Where the road climbs left, turn right and cross a stile. Bear left downhill using stiles to follow the route. Climb a stile and turn right along the main road for 300 yards (275 m) as far as the bend.*

8 *Turn left over the stile. Do not go into the valley, but turn left towards the top of a small wood. Bear right on a grassy path parallel to, and below, the main road. Climb a stile on the left of another clump of trees and follow a grassy depression to the left of a ruined wall. Cross an open field to a ruin by a third clump.*

9 *Turn left away from the ruin uphill to a signpost. Turn right, downhill along a grassy path and into a wooded valley. Cross the stream and climb up to the road.*

10 *Turn right and follow the road across the dam wall to the car park.*

entrance tells the fascinating story of the Goyt Valley.

B Look east along wooded Fernilee Reservoir towards Wild Moor and Burbage Edge. After descending Bunsal, the High Peak Railway followed the valley to the High Peak Canal at Whaley, thereby connecting it across the dry limestone plateau of the White Peak to the Cromford Canal near Matlock.

Walk 30

GOYT'S MOSS

$5\frac{1}{2}$ **miles (9 km) Moderate, NOT SUITABLE IN MIST**

This is a high moorland walk around Burbage Edge and overlooking Buxton. The walk starts in the narrow, wooded, upper reaches of the Goyt Valley, and climbs the heather moor of Goyt's Moss by a pleasantly graded path. On the descent, part of the long-abandoned High Peak Railway is crossed.

Access is by the one-way system along the Goyt Valley. The road is closed to vehicular traffic on busy summer weekends when it will be necessary to park by the reservoir and walk along the valley road. At all other times, park at Goytsclough Quarry.

10 *Where the track climbs left at a waymark post, turn right. Follow a wall around the hillside and across a side valley. Go round another spur and above woodland lining the main valley. Turn right and go down to the bridge, then climb to Goytsclough Quarry.*

9 *Turn left and cross a girder bridge. Follow the track ahead then right, waymarked No. 6.*

8 *Go diagonally right across the old railway. Follow posts downhill on the right-hand side of the valley.*

7 *Turn left at the cream-washed house, uphill at the side of a wood, then left and right towards the moor. Line up posts to follow the faint path.*

1 *Go down to the stream opposite the quarry and over the stone-arched bridge. Turn left up the bracken-covered hillside, then right towards the moor following waymarked path No. 6.*

2 *Bear left and climb the side valley.*

6 *Keep to the left of the farmhouse, then go to the right down its access lane. Turn left at the junction and follow the fenced drive.*

3 *Turn left at a fork marked by a prominent cairn and go over the moorland crest. Cross a stile and go half-right, downhill between the arms of adjacent woodlands.*

5 *Turn left at the fingerpost and follow the access lane as far as the farm. Go through the yard and over stiles to the right of the cottage. Follow a field and woodland path.*

4 *Cross the stile and turn left along a steadily improving road past houses.*

A It is hard to imagine that Pickfords' mighty transport company began by carrying stone from Goytsclough Quarry in the seventeenth century. The stone-arched bridge below was moved there when the Errwood Dam was built.

B Look across the heather moors of Goyt's Moss.

C The bridge crosses the abandoned High Peak Railway on the last of its upland sections before it entered Burbage Tunnel and descended Bunsal Incline.

D Buxton is below in its sheltering hollow. The prominent dome in the town centre is the Devonshire Hospital, once a riding school. To your left, the stepped slopes above Corbar Woods lead to Combs Moss.

E Look across Errwood Reservoir and the secluded valley where the Grimshaws built their mansion in Victorian times.

58

Walk 31

HARROP BROOK

5 miles (8 km) Easy/Moderate

Part of the route follows the Gritstone Trail, a long-distance footpath from Lyme Park to Rushton Spencer. The waymark symbol is a yellow boot superimposed with a brown letter G.

Limited parking can usually be found on the verge at the junction of the A5002 Macclesfield to Whaley Bridge road, and the side road to Pott Shrigley.

1 Turn left from the road below Brink Farm and follow a field track round the brow of the hill. Keep to the left of the old quarry.

2 Cross a stile and go over a cattle grid, then bear left away from the track to follow a stone wall downhill.

3 Bear left below a wood. Go over an access lane and keep to the left of a farm, downhill to a small pond. Cross a stile and bear left downhill; then go through mixed woodland.

4 Cross a narrow footbridge and walk uphill across the next field towards the Cheshire Hunt Inn.

5 Climb a stile and turn left along the lane by the inn.

6 Turn right opposite an asbestos hut. Climb steps up to and over a stile. Bear left uphill.

7 Keep to the right, uphill of an old farmhouse and as far as a stile. Cross into the next field and follow an easier-angled path around the hillside.

8 Go through a metal gate and turn left uphill along the road to a T-junction, and turn left.

9 Opposite the Highwayman Inn, turn left and go past a stone barn. Follow the field track, curving downhill beside walls and then a hawthorn hedge.

10 Cross stiles on either side of an access lane and follow the hedge towards a farm on the left of a belt of trees.

11 Keep to the right in the farmyard and go through a metal gate. Follow a wall pointing to a farm across the valley. Cross the stream and climb, fairly steeply to your left of a wooded side gully.

12 Keep left and go to the right through the farmyard. Follow the access track uphill to the hill-top road. Turn left or right to reach your car.

Gritstone Trail

Bakestonedale Farm

Andrew's Knob 350

B 5470

Berristall Hall

Further Harrop Farm

Harrop Brook

Bollington

PH

Winterside Farm

Harrop Fold Farm

Billinge Head Farm

Withinlow Farm PH

Black Brook

B 5470

A The low, tree-covered ridge ahead is Nab Head, and far to the right is Greater Manchester with its not (from this distance) unattractive city-centre skyline. Aircraft can usually be seen on their final approach and take-off to and from Manchester Airport. The curious white tower on the ridge to your left is called White Nancy and, in the distance, you can probably see the radio telescope of Jodrell Bank.

B The headwaters of Harrop Brook make an attractive scene. Shaly heaps beside the path are the remains of small coal pits, probably worked towards the end of the last century.

Walk 32
TEGG'S NOSE

0   1 mile

0   1 km

5 miles (8 km) Moderate; 492-foot (150-m) descent and ascent

Starting in an area of abandoned gritstone quarries which are now the central feature of a country park about 2 miles (3¼ km) east of Macclesfield, the walk crosses a deep valley and returns by way of Macclesfield Forest. Approach via the Old Macclesfield Road signposted off the A537.

Guided walks leave the car park information centre, and a leaflet is available for the area. Notice the recumbent statue of the mythical giant Tegga, after whom the area is named.

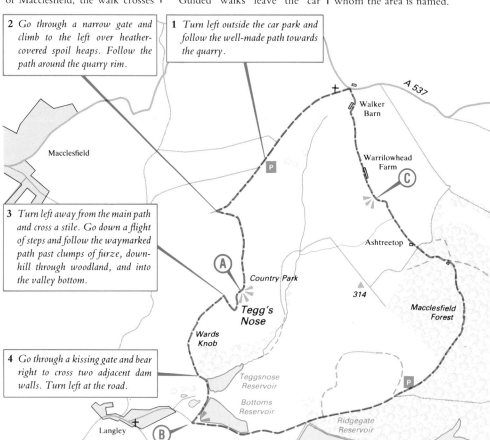

2 *Go through a narrow gate and climb to the left over heather-covered spoil heaps. Follow the path around the quarry rim.*

1 *Turn left outside the car park and follow the well-made path towards the quarry.*

3 *Turn left away from the main path and cross a stile. Go down a flight of steps and follow the waymarked path past clumps of furze, downhill through woodland, and into the valley bottom.*

4 *Go through a kissing gate and bear right to cross two adjacent dam walls. Turn left at the road.*

A 537

Walker Barn

Macclesfield

Warrilowhead Farm

P

C

Ashtreetop

A

Country Park

314

Macclesfield Forest

Tegg's Nose

Wards Knob

Teggsnose Reservoir

Bottoms Reservoir

P

Ridgegate Reservoir

Langley

B

A Langley Reservoir is backed by the dense mass of Macclesfield Forest. Topping it all is the graceful cone of Shutlingsloe – 1660 feet (506 m) – Cheshire's Matterhorn. A nearby exhibition displays stone-cutting and quarrying machinery together with examples of stone walling and masonry techniques.

A yellow boot waymark superimposed by a brown letter G indicates that this part of the walk is following the Gritstone Trail.

Over

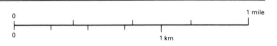

0   1 mile

0   1 km

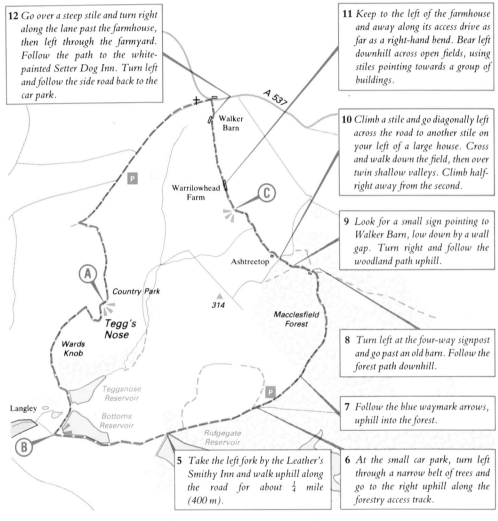

12 *Go over a steep stile and turn right along the lane past the farmhouse, then left through the farmyard. Follow the path to the white-painted Setter Dog Inn. Turn left and follow the side road back to the car park.*

11 *Keep to the left of the farmhouse and away along its access drive as far as a right-hand bend. Bear left downhill across open fields, using stiles pointing towards a group of buildings.*

10 *Climb a stile and go diagonally left across the road to another stile on your left of a large house. Cross and walk down the field, then over twin shallow valleys. Climb half-right away from the second.*

9 *Look for a small sign pointing to Walker Barn, low down by a wall gap. Turn right and follow the woodland path uphill.*

8 *Turn left at the four-way signpost and go past an old barn. Follow the forest path downhill.*

7 *Follow the blue waymark arrows, uphill into the forest.*

6 *At the small car park, turn left through a narrow belt of trees and go to the right uphill along the forestry access track.*

5 *Take the left fork by the Leather's Smithy Inn and walk uphill along the road for about $\frac{1}{4}$ mile (400 m).*

A 537

Walker Barn

Warrilowhead Farm

Ⓒ

Ashtreetop

Ⓐ

Country Park

314

Tegg's Nose

Macclesfield Forest

Ⓟ

Wards Knob

Ⓟ

Teggsnose Reservoir

Bottoms Reservoir

Langley

Ridgegate Reservoir

Ⓑ

B Langley Reservoirs are visited by a large and varied number of wildfowl.

C Tegg's Nose is in front with Langley Reservoirs in the valley bottom. Beyond and to the left is Sutton Common and its strangely adorned telecommunications tower. In the far distance you can probably see Mow Cop in Staffordshire. A folly in the shape of a ruined castle adorns the summit.

61

Walk 33

SUTTON COMMON

$4\frac{1}{4}$ miles (7 km) Easy/Moderate; one climb of 679 feet (207 m)

Sutton Common is just outside the western boundary of the National Park and is one of the highest points of Cheshire. The Gritstone Way is followed for part of the route along a broad, airy ridge above a pleasantly wooded valley. Approach from Macclesfield along the Cleulow Cross road, and park in a small layby at the start of the walk near the Ryle's Arms Inn.

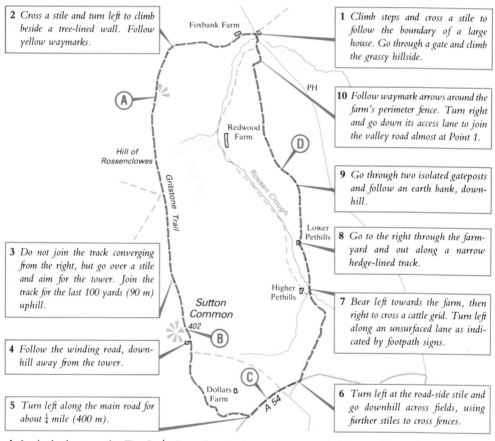

2 Cross a stile and turn left to climb beside a tree-lined wall. Follow yellow waymarks.

Foxbank Farm

1 Climb steps and cross a stile to follow the boundary of a large house. Go through a gate and climb the grassy hillside.

PH

A

Redwood Farm

D

10 Follow waymark arrows around the farm's perimeter fence. Turn right and go down its access lane to join the valley road almost at Point 1.

Hill of Rossenclowes

Gritstone Trail

Rossen Clough

9 Go through two isolated gateposts and follow an earth bank, down-hill.

Lower Pethills

3 Do not join the track converging from the right, but go over a stile and aim for the tower. Join the track for the last 100 yards (90 m) uphill.

Sutton Common
402

Higher Pethills

B

8 Go to the right through the farm-yard and out along a narrow hedge-lined track.

7 Bear left towards the farm, then right to cross a cattle grid. Turn left along an unsurfaced lane as indicated by footpath signs.

4 Follow the winding road, down-hill away from the tower.

C

Dollars Farm

A 54

5 Turn left along the main road for about $\frac{1}{4}$ mile (400 m).

6 Turn left at the road-side stile and go downhill across fields, using further stiles to cross fences.

A Look back towards Tegg's Nose and the line of the Gritstone Way path. On the right are the Goyt Valley moors.

B From the telecommunications tower, the wide-ranging view takes in the southern portion of the Dark Peak, and the craggy ramparts of the Roaches on the right point the way to the White Peak.

C The national park boundary follows the road at this point, but includes the two small fields opposite for some strange reason.

D Earth banks at this point are ancient field boundaries.

Walk 34

CUMBERLAND CLOUGH

6 miles (9½ km) Moderate; boggy sections

This is an easy-to-follow moorland walk from the second highest Inn in England (the highest is the Tan Hill Inn between Swaledale and Teesdale). Joined by Cumberland Clough, the walk continues along the pleasant Wildboarclough valley, in marked contrast with the wildness of the open moor. Parts of the moorland Path can be boggy, especially after prolonged rain. Park opposite the Cat and Fiddle at the highest point on the A537 Buxton to Macclesfield road.

7 Even though there is an access lane ahead from the farm, the Right of Way is a footpath to the left of the drive. Go through the farmyard and turn left along the path. Go over a stile and turn right to follow the road uphill past the farm entrance.

8 Turn right for a few yards at the junction with the main road. Bear left past the Shining Tor Restaurant and ahead on a grassy track.

9 Continue ahead at the track junction. Bear left on reaching the A537 and follow it back to the Cat and Fiddle.

6 Go through a farmyard and continue along the lane. Turn left to cross the stream and climb up to a barn. Bear right, along the footpath following a wall.

1 Follow the moorland footpath directly opposite the Cat and Fiddle Inn.

Torgate Farm
Chest Hollow
Clough Brook
Broughsplace
530
Cat & Fiddle (PH)
A 537
C
A
B

2 Turn right by the signpost and go steeply down to the narrow valley.

5 Opposite the road junction, turn right and cross a bridge. Fork left and follow a stream-side farm lane uphill.

Clough House
Danethorn Hollow
A 54
Cumberland Clough

3 Join a track from the left and walk down the steadily improving path above a tree-lined stream.

4 Go past farm buildings and down the access drive. Turn right along the valley road.

A Look across the moor to the graceful heights of Shutlingsloe above the deep trough of Wildboarclough. The last wild boar is said to have been killed near here but, because there is no factual record, we must assume that, like all other similar folk stories, it is simply a myth.

B Look south over the Dane Valley to the Roaches escarpment and Hen Cloud. Beyond them are the rolling southern uplands of the Peak District.

C The firm, grassy track on the left leads into the Goyt Valley and the ruins of Errwood Hall. (See Walks 29 and 30.)

Walk 35

DANEBRIDGE

$4\frac{1}{4}$ miles (7 km) Easy/Moderate

```
0                                    1 mile
|----------|----------|----------|----------|
0                         1 km
```

There is no record of any Danes living here; the word is Middle Welsh, *dafn*, for a trickling stream. This is an apt description of this secretive and densely wooded valley lying below unspoilt heather moorlands of the Roaches Estate.

Parking is limited to the roadside above the Wincle end of the bridge. Approach along a side road to Wincle from the A54 Buxton to Congleton road.

---

7 *Keep left again at the next farm. Cross the access track and go downhill on a wide grassy path leading to a wood. Beyond the wood, cross a small meadow and follow the riverside path back to Danebridge*

6 *Keep to the left of the old farmhouse, then ahead along a field path.*

5 *Go down to, but not over the footbridge. Turn left and follow the waymarked woodland valley path signposted to Danebridge.*

Back Dane

River Dane

Black Brook

Gradbach

D

C

E

Hanging Stone

330

B

Hangingstone Farm

4 *Take the left fork at the rocks, downhill along the woodland path.*

Danebridge **A**

1 *Walk up the road for about 50 yards (45 m) and, opposite the chapel, turn left. Climb the narrow path between houses signposted to Roach End and Gradbach. Follow the waymarked woodland path to the upper fields.*

2 *Keep to the left of the farm as indicated by waymarks. Cross a stile and turn right along the farm track.*

3 *Pass a second farmhouse and walk along the walled track. Go over a stile and turn left uphill through the gap in the moorland ridge. Bear right, then cross a stile. Follow the path signposted to Gradbach.*

A The Hanging Stone is well named; it projects over the hillside like the barrel of a gun.

B The Dane Valley is below and to the left is Wildboarclough headed by Shutlingsloe. You might see wallabies on the nearby moors, descendants of a herd released from a private zoo during World War 2.

C Look towards the headwaters of the Dane and the moorland village of Flash, once the home of counterfeiters.

D Lud's Church is a natural moorland ravine reached by a short diversion along the right-hand path. Walter de Ludank and other fourteenth-century followers of Wyclif are said to have worshipped here in secret.

E Gradbach, once a silk mill, is now a Youth Hostel.

BARTHOLOMEW WALKS SERIES

Designed to meet the requirements of both experienced and inexperienced walkers, the guides in this series are ideal for anyone who enjoys exploring on foot. They describe the best routes across our greatest walking country from Inverness to the New Forest and Cork & Kerry.

● In each guide, there are at least 30 carefully chosen, easy-to-follow walks over rights of way, with detailed route descriptions accompanying special maps.

● Country walks are graded according to distance and terrain and start from a convenient parking area. The route always returns to the car park, usually by a circular walk and, where appropriate, access by public transport is also possible.

● Notes on local history, geography and wildlife add interest to the walks and the unique notebook format is especially easy to use.

EXPLORE THE BROADS
0 7028 0772 9 £3·50

WALK CORK & KERRY
0 7028 0949 7 £4·95

WALK THE CORNISH COASTAL PATH
A special format step-by-step guide to the entire length of the Cornish Coastal Path (Marsland Mouth - Cremyll).
0 7028 0902 0 £4·95

WALK THE COTSWOLDS
0 7028 0908 X £4·95

WALK THE DALES
0 7028 0800 8 £4·95

MORE WALKS IN THE DALES
0 7028 0948 9 £4·95

YORKSHIRE DALES VISITOR'S PACK
Containing a copy of *Walk the Dales* and a folded 1 inch map of the Yorkshire Dales in a clear, plastic carrying wallet.
0 7028 0932 2 £6·95

WALK DARTMOOR
0 7028 0688 9 £3·95

WALK DORSET & HARDY'S WESSEX
0 7028 0906 3 £3·95

WALK EXMOOR & THE QUANTOCKS
0 7028 0910 1 £3·95

WALK HERTS & BUCKS
0 7028 0953 5 £4·95

WALK THE LAKES
0 7028 8111 2 £3·95

MORE WALKS IN THE LAKES
0 7028 0819 9 £4·95

LAKE DISTRICT WALKING PACK
Containing a copy of *Walk the Lakes* and a folded 1 inch map of the Lake District in a clear, plastic carrying wallet.
0 7028 0876 8 £6·95

WALK LOCH LOMOND & THE TROSSACHS
0 7028 0744 3 £4·95

WALK LOCH NESS & THE RIVER SPEY
0 7028 0787 7 £3·95

BARTHOLOMEW WALKS SERIES (Contd)

WALK THE PEAK DISTRICT
0 7028 0710 9   £4·95

MORE WALKS IN THE PEAK DISTRICT
0 7028 0951 9   £4·95

WALK PERTHSHIRE
0 7028 0766 4   £3·95

**WALK ROYAL DEESIDE
& NORTH EAST SCOTLAND**
0 7028 0898 9   £3·95

WALK LONDON
0 7028 0771 0   £3·95

WALK SNOWDONIA & NORTH WALES
0 7028 0804 0   £3·95

WALK LOTHIAN, THE BORDERS & FIFE
0 7028 0803 2   £3·95

WALK THE SOUTH DOWNS
0 7028 0811 3   £3·95

WALK THE NEW FOREST
0 7028 0810 5   £4·95

WALK THE SOUTH PENNINES
0 7028 0955 1   £4·95

WALK THE NORTH DOWNS
0 7028 0742 7   £3·95

**WALK SOUTH WALES
& THE WYE VALLEY**
0 7028 0904 7   £3·95

WALK THE NORTH YORK MOORS
0 7028 0743 5   £3·95

WALK NORTHUMBRIA
0 7028 0959 4   £4·95

WALK SOUTH WEST SCOTLAND
0 7028 0900 4   £3·95

WALK OBAN, MULL & LOCHABER
0 7028 0801 6   £3·95

WALK THE THAMES & CHILTERNS
0 7028 0802 4   £3·95

Guides in this series may be purchased from good bookshops. In the event of difficulty copies may be obtained by post. *Please send your order with your remittance to*
**BARTHOLOMEW BOOKSERVICE BY POST,
PO BOX 29, DOUGLAS, ISLE OF MAN, BRITISH ISLES.**

NAME _____

ADDRESS _____

_____

_____

Please enclose a cheque or postal order made out to 'Bartholomew' for the amount due and allow 25 pence per book postage & packing fee up to a maximum of £3.00.
While every effort is made to keep prices low, it is sometimes necessary to increase cover prices at short notice.
Bartholomew reserves the right to show new retail prices on covers which may differ from those previously advertised in the text or elsewhere.